T0298058

Positive POWERFUL *Promotional* Words

ACKNOWLEDGMENTS

General Assistance and Motivation: Don Surbeck, Shari Surbeck-Hirsch, David and Lisa Surbeck, Lee Surbeck, Eddie Niccolls

Editing: Bill Butler

Cover Design: Jack Jeffries

Published Summer, 1997 by Master Publications, Inc., 10331 Linn Station Road, Louisville, Kentucky 40223.

Library of Congress Number

ISBN 0-9628820-3-8

DEDICATION

The concept for **Positive POWERFUL *Promotional* Words** originated in my mind some twenty years ago after having read several books by Norman Vincent Peale on positive thinking. I believed his approach to looking at life in a positive manner would make life easier, happier and more rewarding for ourselves and those around us.

I became a faithful student of Reverend Peale, as well as one of his protégés, Reverend Robert Schuller. Dr. Schuller also wrote many "positive" books while creating and maintaining "The Hour Of Power," which I have watched "religiously" for years. I know these great men have contributed significantly to my personal and mental well-being.

Moving to a Higher Source of recognition for my spirit and all that I am, and in appreciation for those I love, I dedicate this book to our POSITIVE and POWERFUL GOD!

HOW TO USE THIS BOOK

This book is a resource for **Positive POWERFUL *Promotional* Words**. It is presented in such a way that, as you search for *the perfect word*, you may find *many* effective ways to fine-tune your message and structure your communication in a positive, powerful or promotional manner.

Words are listed alphabetically from A to Z. Each was selected for its Positive, Powerful or Promotional definition. You will note that in a few cases, certain words could carry a meaning unfitting the title of this book, but with imagination, desire, and a little twist, a positive implication could be found. This approach supports the underlying message of the book: "You can find a good meaning in anything, if you look for it!"

Each word's grammatical identification is determined, followed by its definition. In most cases, a series of synonyms or alternate words with similar meanings is listed. This extensive grouping will stimulate new ideas and therefore a great opportunity to find the *perfect word*.

The final section was developed to give a more elaborate list of alternatives for the words used routinely; MOST OFTEN USED Words.

Generous spacing has been purposely allotted in this book in order to allow the mind to wander, using creativity to search for the most appropriate word for any context.

Please use this book with an open mind and with joy, knowing others will appreciate and respond positively to your message, verbal or written, if it is told with **Positive POWERFUL *Promotional* Words**.

ABOUT THE AUTHOR

Linda Surbeck is an entrepreneur. She currently owns and operates three businesses. All are PROMOTIONAL in nature and all require POSITIVE copy writing. They are:

~ **MASTER OF CEREMONIES** ~ a full service event production firm.

~ **FESTÍVA INTERNATIONÁLE** ~ an event marketing and sponsorship firm.

~ **MASTER PUBLICATIONS** ~ a publishing company specializing in the art and science of special events, promotions, and communications.

Speaking engagements, civic activities, and serving on the boards of many professional organizations are also part of her business schedule. She is the author of ***CREATING SPECIAL EVENTS: The Ultimate Guide to Producing Successful Events,*** an internationally acclaimed industry book.

Linda knows her source of support is God, her family, great friends and associates. Her church is a very important part of her life.

She believes success is powered by a POSITIVE attitude, and that the world would be much happier if we all would use a book like this to speak a fluent language of **Positive POWERFUL *Promotional* Words**.

A-Z Defined Words & Options

A-Z

....

Defined Words & Options

A

ABILITY	ADMIRE	ALLURE
ABOUNDING	ADMIT	ALMIGHTY
ABOVE	ADMITTANCE	ALOFT
ABREAST	ADOPT	ALOUD
ABSOLUTE	ADORE	ALREADY
ABSORB	ADROIT	ALSO
ABUNDANT	ADVANCE	ALTOGETHER
ACCELERATE	ADVANTAGE	ALWAYS
ACCENTUATE	ADVENTURE	AMAZE
ACCEPT	ADVERTISE	AMBASSADOR
ACCESSION	ADVISABLE	AMBIANCE
ACCESSORY	ADVOCATE	AMBITION
ACLAIM	AESTHETIC	AMEN
ACCOLADE	AFFABLE	AMENITY
ACCOMODATE	AFFECT	AMIABLE
ACCOMPLISH	AFFECTION	AMPLE
ACCORD	AFFINITY	AMPLIFY
ACCRUE	AFFIRM	ANEW
ACCURATE	AFFLUENT	ANGEL
ACE	AFFORD	ANNEX
ACHIEVE	AFRESH	ANNOUNCE
ACKNOWLEDGE	AGAIN	ANNUAL
ACQUAINT	AGELESS	ANOTHER
ACQUIESCENCE	AGENT	ANTICIPATE
ACQUIRE	AGILE	APEX
ACTIVE	AGOG	APHORISM
ACTUAL	AGREEMENT	APLOMB
ACUTE	AID	APPEAL
AD	AIM	APPEAR
ADAGE	ALACRITY	APPEASE
ADAPT	ALERT	APPEND
ADD	ALIVE	APPLAUSE
ADDRESS	ALL	APPLICATION
ADEPT	ALLAY	APPOINT
ADEQUATE	ALLEGIANCE	APPRECIATE
ADHERE (to)	ALLELUIA	APPRISE
ADJUSTABLE	ALLIANCE	APPROACH
ADMINISTER	ALLOW	APPROACHABLE

A

APPROVE
APPROPRIATE
APT
APTITUDE
ARRANGE
ARRAY
ARRIVE
ART
ASCEND
ASK
ASPIRE
ASSEMBLY
ASSENT
ASSERT
ASSESS
ASSET
ASSIDUOUS
ASSIGN
ASSIST
ASSOCIATE
ASSORTMENT
ASSUAGE

ASSUME
ASSURANCE
ASTONISH
ATTACHMENT
ATTAIN
ATTEMPT
ATTEST
ATTITUDE
ATTRACT
ATTRACTIVE
ATTRIBUTE
ATTUNE
AUDIENCE
AUGMENT
AUTHORITY
AVANT-GARDE
AVER
AWARD
AWARE
AWE
AYE

ABILITY *(noun)*

the quality that makes an action or process possible; the capacity or power to do something; cleverness; talent.

Optional Words:

ableness	capability	capacity	competence
faculty	might	adeptness	command
craft	expertise	expertness	knack
know-how	mastery	proficiency	skill
efficiency			

ABOUNDING *(adjective)*

to be plentiful; to have in great quantities; to exist in large numbers.

Optional Words:

overflowing	swarming	rich	stuffed
teeming	filled	wealthy	
replete	rife	jammed	

ABOVE *(adjective)*

at or to a higher point; overhead; in heaven; in addition; earlier in a book or article; over; higher than; more than; upstream from; beyond the level or reach of; carried away by high spirits or conceit; more important than.

Optional Words:

superior to	beyond	over	overhead
better than	elevated	aloft	

ABREAST *(adverb)*

side-by-side and facing the same way; keeping up.

Optional Words:

acquainted	au courant	versed	contemporary
familiar	informed	up-to-date	versant

A

ABSOLUTE *(adjective)*

free from imperfection, mixture, restraint, or limitation.

Optional Words:

perfect	pure	utter	consummate
factual	categorical	sheer	complete
simple	clear	ideal	

ABSORB *(verb)*

to take in; to combine or merge into itself or oneself to incorporate; soak up; to occupy the full attention of.

Optional Words:

assimilate	consume	digest	engross
immerse	imbibe	preoccupy	monopolize
engage			

ABUNDANT *(adjective)*

more than enough; plentiful; having plenty of something; rich.

Optional Words:

generous	prosperous	thriving	bounteous
profuse			

ACCELERATE *(verb)*

to move faster or happen earlier or more quickly.

Optional Words:

hasten	hurry	impel	quicken
step up	drive	speed up	

ACCENTUATE *(verb)*

to emphasize; point out.

Optional Words:

accent	stress	highlight

ACCEPT *(verb)*

to take willingly; to say yes to an offer or invitation; to undertake.

Optional Words:

embrace	take up	welcome	admit
receive	take in	agree	understand
assent	believe	grasp	comprehend

ACCESSION *(noun)*

reaching a rank, office, or position; an addition.

Optional Words:

accretion	increase	increment	augmentation
raise	rise		

ACCESSORY *(adjective)*

additional; extra.

Optional Words:

adjunct	auxillary	ancillary	collateral
contributory			

(noun)

something extra or useful or decorative but not essential.

Optional Words:

addition	appendage	appendix	accompaniment

A

ACCLAIM *(verb)*

to welcome with shouts of approval; to applaud enthusiastically; to praise.

Optional Words:

honor	compliment	commend	hail
cheer	laud		

(noun)

applause or praise.

Optional Words:

reverence	plaudits	homage	recognition

ACCOLADE *(noun)*

praise; approval; a ceremonial tap on the shoulder with the flat of a sword given when a knighthood is conferred.

Optional Words:

distinction	honor	award	badge
kudo	decoration	laurel	commendation

ACCOMMODATE *(verb)*

to do as one is asked; to do a favor for; to help.

Optional Words:

oblige	adjust	fit	tailor
adopt	conform	square	reconcile
integrate			

ACCOMPLISH *(verb)*

to succeed in doing; to fulfill.

Optional Words:

finish	achieve	attain	gain
reach	realize	score	win
actualize	arrive	complete	conquer

ACCORD *(noun)*

an agreement between parties.

Optional Words:
harmony   **treaty**   **unanimity**   **conformance**
grant   **concordance**

ACCRUE *(verb)*

to come about as a natural increase or addition; to accumulate over time.

Optional Words:
grow   **accumulate** **increase**   **enlarge**

ACCURATE *(adjective)*

free from error; conforming exactly to a standard or to truth.

Optional Words:
correct   **exact**   **precise**   **proper**
right   **rigorous**

ACE *(noun)*

a person who excels at something.

Optional Words:
expert

Defined Words and Options
Page 7

A

ACHIEVE *(verb)*

to accomplish; to gain or reach by effort.

Optional Words:

attain   **reach**   **finish**   **realize**

ACKNOWLEDGE *(verb)*

to recognize or admit that something is true or valid.

Optional Words:

allow   **avow**   **concede**   **confess**
grant   **proclaim**

ACQUIESCENCE *(noun)*

acceptance; agreement.

Optional Words:

compliance   **conformity**

ACQUAINT *(verb)*

to make aware or familiar.

Optional Words:

introduce   **present**   **accustom**   **inform**
advise   **appraise**

ACQUIRE *(verb)*

to gain possession of.

Optional Words:

get	accomplish	annex	obtain
procure	land		

ACTIVE *(adjective)*

producing action or movement.

Optional Words:

alive	functioning	going	live
operative	running	vigorous	

ACTUAL *(adjective)*

existing in fact.

Optional Words:

indisputable	real	true	absolute
factual	hard	genuine	positive
concrete	tangible	authentic	

ACUTE *(adjective)*

(in humans) very perceptive; having a sharp mind.

Optional Words:

keen	sensitive	incisive	pointed
sharp			

A

AD *(noun)*

diminutive for an advertisement.

Optional Words:
**broadcast declaration proclamation announcement
promulgation publication pronouncement
spot (broadcast)**

ADAGE *(noun)*

an old saying.

Optional Words:
**byword saying word proverb
aphorism maxim**

ADAPT *(verb)*

to make or become suitable for a new use or situation.

Optional Words:
**adjust acclimate conform accommodate
fashion fit reconcile square
suit tailor**

ADD *(verb)*

to join, increase or supplement.

Optional Words:
**accumulate annex append plus
combine**

ADDRESS *(noun)*

a speech delivered to an audience.

Optional Words:

talk (to)	**lecture**	**appeal (to)**	**apply (to)**
approach	**petition**	**speak**	

ADEPT *(adjective)*

very skillful, proficient.

Optional Words:

expert	**able**	**talented**	**professional**
competent	**crack**	**crackerjack**	**virtuoso**
adroit			

ADEQUATE *(adjective)*

sufficient, satisfactory.

Optional Words:

comfortable	**enough**	**satisfactory**	**sufficing**

ADHERE (to) *(verb)*

to remain faithful; to continue to give one's support.

Optional Words:

follow	**bind**	**confine**	**join**
link	**unite**		

Defined Words and Options
Page 11

A

ADJUSTABLE *(adjective)*

able to be adjusted.

Optional Words:

adaptable   conforming   fitting   accommodating
fixable

ADMINISTER *(verb)*

to give or hand out as deserved; to oversee.

Optional Words:

direct	govern	head	superintend
manage	run	execute	dispense
give (out)	provide		

ADMIRE *(verb)*

to regard with pleasure, satisfaction or approval.

Optional Words:

approve of	appreciate	enjoy	relish
consider	esteem	honor	regard
respect	value		

ADMIT *(verb)*

accept as true or valid.

Optional Words:

permit	allow	avow	acknowledge
concede	confess	grant	assent
agree	subscribe	recognize	

ADMITTANCE *(noun)*

being allowed to enter.

Optional Words:

admission   access   entree

ADOPT *(verb)*

to approve or accept; take and make one's own.

Optional Words:

embrace   espouse   take on   take up

ADORE *(verb)*

to love deeply; to delight in.

Optional Words:

idolize   revere   venerate   worship
love   delight in   groove on *(slang)*

(noun)

to decorate with ornaments; to add something to enhance appearance or beauty.

Optional Words:

grace   bedeck   deck (out)   dress (up)
trim   embellish   garnish   furbish
spruce up   enrich   enhance

ADROIT *(adjective)*

skillful; expert; ingenious.

Optional Words:

artful   dexterous   clever   deft
handy   nimble   astute   adept

A

ADVANCE *(verb)*

to move or put forward; to make progress.

Optional Words:
encourage foster   promote

ADVANTAGE *(noun)*

a favorable condition, circumstance or position.

Optional Words:
head start   leg up   benefit   gain

ADVENTURE *(noun)*

an exciting or new experience.

Optional Words:
enterprise   venture   feat   quest

ADVERTISE *(verb)*

to make generally or publicly known; to notify.

Optional Words:
plug	promote	publicize	spread the word
push	talk up	broadcast	announce
ballyhoo	report	blazon	communicate
proclaim	herald		

ADVISABLE *(adjective)*

worth recommending as a course of action.

Optional Words:

reasonable	prudent	wise	recommendable

ADVOCATE *(verb)*

to strongly recommend.

Optional Words:

support	back	back up	champion
side (with)	uphold	promote	advance
urge	further	push	bolster

AESTHETIC *(adjective)*

artistic, tasteful.

Optional Words

creative	beautiful	appreciative

AFFABLE *(adjective)*

polite and friendly.

Optional Words:

amiable	gracious	congenial	cordial
sociable	courteous	suave	genial

A

AFFECT *(verb)*

to touch or move emotionally.

Optional Words:

impress	influence	instill	sway
touch	stimulate	inspire	

AFFECTION *(noun)*

a strong liking.

Optional Words:

fondness	fancy	attachment	friendship
love	feeling	emotion	passion
sentiment	devotion		

AFFINITY *(noun)*

a strong natural liking or attraction.

Optional Words:

likeness	sympathy	analogy	comparison
similarity	resemblance		

AFFIRM *(verb)*

to assert; to state as a fact.

Optional Words:

confirm	aver	declare	profess
certify	state	guarantee	witness
say	prove	assert	repeat
insist			

• •

AFFLUENT *(adjective)*

rich; wealthy.

Optional Words:
ample   opulent   abundant   substantial
prosperous   comfortable

AFFORD *(verb)*

to have enough money, means or time for a specified purpose.

AFRESH *(adverb)*

anew; beginning again.

Optional Words:
over   revived   once more

AGAIN *(adverb)*

another time; once more.

Optional Words:
anew   afresh   over

A

AGELESS *(adjective)*

not growing or appearing old.

Optional Words:

dateless   eternal   timeless   intemporal

AGENT *(noun)*

one who acts on behalf of another.

Optional Words:

means   channel   vehicle   delegate
assignee   proctor

AGILE *(adjective)*

nimble; quickly moving; acting or moving with easy alacrity.

Optional Words:

active   brisk   lively   sprightly
spry   zippy

AGOG *(adjective)*

full of interest and excitement.

Optional Words:

ardent   avid   breathless   eager
impatient   keen   expectant

AGREEMENT *(noun)*

harmony of opinion or feeling.

Optional Words:

accordance **concord** **conformity** **correspondence**
conformance conformation **confirmation**

AID *(noun)*

help; assistance.

Optional Words:

comfort **hand** **lift** **relief**
succor **support**

AIM *(verb)*

to point or send toward a target.

Optional Words:

cast **direct** **train (on)** **zero in (on)**
aspire **seek**

ALACRITY *(noun)*

cheerful readiness.

Optional Words:

goodwill **readiness** **briskness** **eagerness**
enthusiasm **fervor** **zeal** **heartiness**
quickness **promptness** **readiness**

A

ALERT *(adjective)*

watchful and ready.

Optional Words:

open-eyed	wakeful	watchful	wide-awake
on guard	vigilant	attentive	heedful
mindful	careful		

ALIVE *(adjective)*

having life; existing.

Optional Words:

vital	animated	active	dynamic
quick	living	alert	bright
spirited			

ALL *(pronoun)*

the whole amount; number or extent; everyone, everything.

(adjective)

the whole of, every one of.

Optional Words:

complete	entire	gross	outright
total	full		

ALLAY *(verb)*

to calm; to put at rest.

Optional Words:

pacify	lighten	relieve	appease
moderate	soothe	compose	quiet
soften	still	tranquilize	alleviate
ease	mitigate	mollify	balm
lull	subdue		

A

ALLEGIANCE *(noun)*

loyalty and/or obedience to a government, sovereign or cause.

Optional Words:

fidelity	loyalty	devotion	faithfulness
ardor	fealty		

ALLELUIA *(interjection & noun)*

praise to God, form of Hallelujah.

Optional Words

glory be	praise be	hurray	hosanna
thank heaven		bless the Lord	

ALLIANCE *(noun)*

a union or association formed for mutual benefit.

Optional Words:

coalition	federation	league	union
affiliation	concord	bond	collaboration
affinity	mutuality	tie	membership

ALLOW *(verb)*

to permit.

Optional Words:

allot	agree	admit	confer
grant	apportion	assign	acknowledge
give	bestow	let	

ALLURE *(verb)*

to entice; to attract.

Optional Words:

bewitch   **captivate**   **charm**   **draw**
enchant   **fascinate**

ALMIGHTY *(adjective)*

all powerful; very great.

Optional Words:

omnipotent

ALOFT *(adverb)*

in the air.

Optional Words:

above   **over**   **overhead**   **upward**

ALOUD *(adverb)*

in a voice loud enough to be heard.

Optional Words:

loud   **audible**

ALREADY *(adverb)*

before this time.

Optional Words:

earlier	**even**	**hereto**	**once**
previously			

ALSO *(adverb)*

in the same manner; in addition; besides.

Optional Words:

additionally	**as well**	**furthermore**	**likewise**
moreover	**still**	**too**	**correspondingly**
withal	**yet**	**similarly**	

ALTOGETHER *(adverb)*

entirely; totally.

Optional Words:

completely	**purely**	**well**	**perfectly**
quite	**right**	**thoroughly**	**utterly**
wholly	**in toto**	**just**	**exactly**

ALWAYS *(adverb)*

at all times.

Optional Words:

constantly	**ever**	**invariably**	**continuously**
perpetually	**forever**	**everlasting**	**ceaselessly**
eternally	**evermore**		

A

AMAZE *(verb)*

to overwhelm with wonder.

Optional Words:

surprise	astonish	marvel	astound
flabbergast			

AMBASSADOR *(noun)*

an official representative.

Optional Words

envoy	minister	consul	agent
emissary	attache'		

AMBIANCE *(noun)*

environment; surroundings.

Optional Words:

atmosphere	climate	medium	milieu

AMBITION *(noun)*

a strong desire to achieve.

Optional Words:

aspiration	aim	goal	mark
object	objective	drive	enterprise
gumption	initiative	passion	craving
energy	vigor	avidity	eagerness
zeal			

AMEN *(interjection)*
so be it.

AMENITY *(noun)*
pleasantness of place or circumstance.
Optional Words:

comfort	facility	luxury	convenience

AMIABLE *(adjective)*
feeling and inspiring friendliness.
Optional Words:

affable	agreeable	cordial	good-natured
easygoing	genial	friendly	good-tempered
complaisant			

AMPLE *(adjective)*
plentiful; quite enough.
Optional Words:

broad	full	generous	commodious
roomy	abundant	copious	liberal
spacious	capacious		

A ●

AMPLIFY *(verb)*

to increase; enlarge.

Optional Words:

elaborate	increase	expand	inflate
augment	extend		

ANEW *(adverb)*

again in a new or different way.

Optional Words:

afresh	again	over	once more
lately	newly	recently	

ANGEL *(noun)*

an attendant or messenger of God; a helper.

Optional Words:

patron	sponsor	backer	guarantor

ANNEX *(verb)*

to add or join to a larger thing.

Optional Words:

link	unite	append	subjoin
take on	join	connect	

A

ANNOUNCE *(verb)*

to make known publicly or officially.

Optional Words:

advertise	enunciate	broadcast	declare
proclaim	publish		

ANNUAL *(adjective)*

coming or happening once every year.

Optional Words

yearly	each year	every year	once a year

ANOTHER *(adjective)*

additional; one more.

Optional Words:

added	else	fresh	further
more	new	other	

ANTICIPATE *(verb)*

to foresee; to expect.

Optional Words:

forecast	predict	prophecy	contemplate
assume	await	prognosticate	

A

APEX *(noun)*

the tip or highest point.

Optional Words:

climax	cusp	tip	prominence
cap	crest	top	crown
peak	roof	summit	zenith
pinnacle			

APHORISM *(noun)*

a short wise saying; a maxim.

Optional Words:

proverb

APLOMB *(noun)*

confidence; flair.

Optional Words:

poise	savoir	ease	nonchalance
easiness	equanimity	coolness	self-confidence
assurance	sa voir faire		

APPEAL *(verb)*

to make an earnest or formal request.

Optional Words:

apply	petition	beg	beseech
implore	plead	play	supplicate

● ●

APPEAR *(verb)*

to become or be visible; to give a certain impression.

Optional Words:

emerge	loom	materialize	show
show up	arrive	come	arise
emanate			

APPEASE *(verb)*

to make calm or quiet by making concessions.

Optional Words:

pacify	satisfy	mollify	placate
ease	gratify	soothe	relieve

APPEND *(verb)*

to attach; to add at the end.

Optional Words:

annex	subjoin	take on	connect
join	unite	link	

APPLAUSE *(noun)*

hand-clapping signifying warm approval.

Optional Words:

ovation	plaudit	cheers	hand
rooting	acclaim	praise	approbation

APPLICATION *(noun)*

putting to use.

Optional Words:

operation	utilization	diligence	implementation
duty	exercise	relevance	administration

APPOINT *(verb)*

to choose for a job or purpose.

Optional Words:

tap	name	nominate	designate
commission			

APPRECIATE *(verb)*

to value greatly.

Optional Words:

cherish	enjoy	esteem	prize
relish	respect	savor	treasure
value	admire	regard	

APPRISE *(verb)*

to inform.

Optional Words:

acquaint	advise	clue	communicate
fill in	notify	post	tell
warn	reveal	disclose	proclaim
publish	announce	declare	

APPROACH *(verb)*

to come near.

Optional Words:

address	start	advance	approximate
near	nigh		

APPROACHABLE *(adjective)*

friendly and easy to talk to.

Optional Words:

accessible	friendly	responsive	warm
welcoming	open		

APPROVE *(verb)*

to agree to.

Optional Words:

accept	approbate	favor	subscribe to
go for	hold with	confirm	pass

APPROPRIATE *(adjective)*

suitable for or belonging to a person, circumstance, or place.

Optional Words:

apt	becoming	befitting	congruous
pertinent	suitable	agreeable	compatible
harmonic	unified	sympathetic	

A

APT *(adjective)*

suitable; inclined; likely.

Optional Words:
**compatible   fluent   like   appropriate
fitting**

APTITUDE *(noun)*

a natural ability or skill.

Optional Words:
talent	**efficiency**	**ableness**	**competence**
adeptness	**tendency**	**drift**	**inclination**

ARRANGE *(verb)*

to put into a certain order.

Optional Words:
array	**assort**	**classify**	**dispose**
distribute	**group**	**marshal**	**order**
organize	**range**	**rank**	**sort**
systematize	**lay out**	**prepare**	**schedule**
work out	**conclude**	**fix**	**negotiate**
settle	**harmonize**		

ARRAY *(verb)*

to display an arrangement of multiple units.

Optional Words:
arrange	**marshal**	**methodize**	**organize**
group	**cluster**	**systematize**	

ARRIVE *(verb)*

to reach one's destination; to be recognized as having achieved success.

Optional Words:

check in	get in	pull in	reach
show up	turn up	accomplish	achieve
succeed			

ART *(noun)*

the production of something beautiful; any practical skill; a knack.

Optional Words:

craft	expertise	know-how	technique
artfulness	artifice	proficiency	finesse
savvy			

ASCEND *(verb)*

to go or come up.

Optional Words:

climb	mount	scale	rise
escalade	escalate		

ASK *(verb)*

to inquire; seek an answer.

Optional Words:

examine	inquire	query	question
quiz	pose	put	raise
demand	request	solicit	exact
beg	bid		

A

ASPIRE *(verb)*

to have an earnest desire or ambition for something high and good; seek after; to reach or rise upward.

Optional Words:

aim (for)	desire	wish	want
dream			

ASSEMBLY *(noun)*

persons gathered together.

Optional Words:

assemblage	body	company	congregation
conclave	congress	crowd	convocation
gathering	group	meeting	muster
convention			

ASSENT *(verb)*

to consent; to express agreement.

Optional Words:

accede	accept	acquiesce	agree
subscribe	say yes	submit	yield

ASSERT *(verb)*

to declare as true.

Optional Words:

affirm	aver	avow	declare
hold	maintain	state	claim
warrant			

A

ASSESS *(verb)*

to determine the amount or value of something.

Optional Words:

estimate	**impose**	**levy**	**enact**
appraise	**evaluate**	**survey**	**deem**
calculate	**weigh**		

ASSET *(noun)*

a property or characteristic that has value.

Optional Words:

resource	**capital**	**wealth**	**equity**
principle			

ASSIDUOUS *(adjective)*

diligent and persevering.

Optional Words:

industrious	**sedulous**	**hardworking**	**tireless**
zealous			

ASSIGN *(verb)*

to allot; to pick for a specific job.

Optional Words:

attribute	**apportion**	**fix**	**station**
transfer			

A

ASSIST *(verb)*

to help.

Optional Words:

aid	assist	comfort	hand
lift	relief	succor	support
back	uphold	abet	relieve
serve			

ASSOCIATE *(noun)*

a partner, colleague, or companion.

Optional Words:

affiliate	ally	cohort	colleague
confederate	copartner	fellow	comrade
mate	friend		

ASSORTMENT *(noun)*

a collection composed of several sorts.

Optional Words:

diversity	variety	medley	conglomeration
pot pourri			

ASSUAGE *(verb)*

to soothe; to make less severe.

Optional Words:

pacify	relieve	placate	appease
allay	alleviate	ease	lighten
mitigate	mollify		

A

ASSUME *(verb)*

to take as true; to take on.

Optional Words:

incur	shoulder	tackle	understand
take over	take up	undertake	appropriate
preempt	affect	act	presume

ASSURANCE *(noun)*

a formal declaration or promise given to inspire confidence.

Optional Words:

confidence	word	guarantee	understanding
pledge	warrant	oath	convenant
pact	certainty		

ASTONISH *(verb)*

to surprise very greatly.

Optional Words:

amaze	astound	dumbfound	flabbergast

ATTACHMENT *(noun)*

physical connection; strong affection.

Optional Words:

affection	bond	fondness	love
loyalty	tie		

A

ATTAIN *(verb)*

to succeed in doing or getting.

Optional Words:

accomplish	arrive at	realize	win
reach	rack up	secure	achieve
gain	score		

ATTEMPT *(verb)*

to make an effort to accomplish.

Optional Words:

assay	endeavor	seek	strive
try	undertake		

ATTEST *(verb)*

to provide clear proof of.

Optional Words:

certify	confirm	indicate	corroborate
testify	vouch	witness	substantiate
uphold	affirm	warrant	support
verify			

ATTITUDE *(noun)*

a way of thinking or behaving.

Optional Words:

position	posture	sentiment	stance
stand			

ATTRACT *(verb)*

to get the attention of.

Optional Words:

allure	appeal	draw	lure
magnetize	pull	enchant	wile
fascinate	charm		

ATTRACTIVE *(adjective)*

pleasing in appearance or effect.

Optional Words:

alluring	appealing	attracting	captivating
charming	enchanting	fascinating	magnetic
tempting	winning	winsome	delightful

ATTRIBUTE *(noun)*

a quality that is a characteristic of a person or thing.

Optional Words:

character	feature	mark	property
trait	virtue	symbol	characteristic
facet	aspect		

ATTUNE *(verb)*

to harmonize or adapt to a matter or idea.

Optional Words:

conform	coordinate	integrate	accommodate
proportion	reconcile	tune	

A

AUDIENCE *(noun)*

persons who have gathered to hear or watch something.

Optional Words:

clientele	public	admirers	devotees
fanciers	fans		

AUGMENT *(verb)*

to add to; to increase.

Optional Words:

build	compound	enlarge	expand
extend	heighten	magnify	multiply

AUTHORITY *(noun)*

the power or right to give orders and make others obey; a person with specialized knowledge.

Optional Words:

clout	command	control	dominion
jurisdiction	mastery	might	power
prerogative	sway	higher-up	official
expert			

AVANT-GARDE *(adjective)*

using or favoring an ultramodern style.

Optional Words:

new	liberal	progressive

A

AVER *(verb)*

to assert; to state as true.

Optional Words:

affirm	avow	declare	depose
predicate	profess	protest	maintain
defend	justify		

AWARD *(verb)*

to give by official decision as a payment or prize.

Optional Words:

confer	grant	accord	give

(noun)

a payment or prize.

Optional Words:

accolade	honor	badge	laurel
kudo			

AWARE *(adjective)*

having knowledge or realization of.

Optional Words:

alive	awake	cognizant	conversant
knowing	mindful	sensible	sentient
wise			

AWE *(noun)*

respect combined with wonder.

Optional Words:

admiration	esteem	regard	amazement
veneration	worship	wonderment	reverence

A

AYE *(adverb)*

    yes.

    (noun)
    a vote in favor of a proposal.
    Optional Words:
    all right   okay   yes

B

Section Index

BACK
BAG
BALL
BAND
BANK (on)
BANTER
BAPTIZE
BASK
BE
BEAM
BEAR
BEAT
BEAUTIFUL
BEAUTIFY
BECKON
BECOME
BECOMING
BEFIT
BEFORE
BEFRIEND
BEGET
BEGIN
BEGUILE
BEHAVE
BEHOLD
BEHOLDEN
BEING
BELIEVE
BELLE
BELLOW
BELONG
BELOVED

BEND
BENEDICTION
BENEFIT
BENIGN
BENISON
BENT
BEQUEATH
BESIDE
BESOTTED
BESPEAK
BEST
BESTOW
BETIDE
BETOKEN
BETROTH
BETTER
BEVY
BEWITCH
BEYOND
BIAS
BIBLE
BICENTENNIAL
BID
BIDDABLE
BIDE
BIENNIAL
BIG
BIJOU
BILLOW
BIND
BLARNEY
BLAZE

BLAZON
BLEND
BLESS
BLISS
BLOSSOM
BODE
BOLD
BOND
BOOM
BOON
BOOST
BOUNCE
BOW
BRACE
BRACING
BRAIN
BRAINSTORM
BRAVE
BRAVO
BRAVURA
BRAWN
BREAK
BREAKTHROUGH
BREEZE
BRIGHT
BRIO
BRISK
BROAD
BUDDY
BULK
BUMPER

B

BACK *(verb)*

to give one's support; assist.

Optional Words:

confirm	support	aid	corroborate
abet	help		

BAG *(verb)*

to take possession of; to stake a claim to.

Optional Words:

take	catch	clench	net
sack	capture	secure	nail

BALL *(noun)*

a social assembly for dancing.

Optional Words:

dance	event

BAND *(verb)*

to unite in an organized group.

Optional Words:

assemble	bind	bunch	cluster
join	unite	amalgamate	combine
concur	team (up)		

B

BANK (on) *(verb)*

to base one's hopes on.

Optional Words:

depend (on)   plan (on)   count (on)   rely (on)

BANTER *(noun)*

good-humored teasing.

Optional Words:

repartee   wit   fun   jest

BAPTIZE *(verb)*

to perform baptism on; to immerse in water or pour water on symbolizing dedication to Christ.

Optional Words:

cleanse   consecrate   sanctify   asperse
christen   immerse   regenerate   purify

BASK *(verb)*

to lie or relax in warmth.

Optional Words:

luxuriate   revel   indulge   wallow

B

BE *(verb)*

to exist; to live.

Optional Words:

subsist	prevail	endure	abide
remain			

BEAM *(noun)*

a ray or stream of light or other radiation.

Optional Words:

ray	shaft	brightness	radiance
brilliance	shine	gleam	

BEAR *(verb)*

to carry; to support.

Optional Words:

abide	endure	sustain	bring forth
produce	shoulder		

BEAT *(verb)*

to do better than.

Optional Words:

conquer	win	prevail	top
triumph	succeed	outdo	excel
better			

B

....

BEAUTIFUL *(adjective)*

very pleasing in appearance or design.

Optional Words:

attractive	lovely	bonny	beauteous
pretty	stunning	choice	well-favored
elegant	exquisite	glorious	resplendent
splendid	sublime	superb	personable
pleasing	handsome	fine	charming
dreamy			

(noun)

having qualities that give pleasure to the senses or to the mind.

Optional Words:

belle	handsome	fine	pretty
lovely	charming	dazzling	eyeful
looker	dreamy	knockout	stunner

BEAUTIFY *(verb)*

to make beautiful.

Optional Words:

adorn	bedeck	decorate	dress (up)
embellish	garnish	ornament	trim
prettify	glamorize		

BECKON *(verb)*

to signal or summon by a gesture.

Optional Words:

direct	entice	lure

BECOME *(verb)*

to come or grow to be; to begin to be.

Optional Words:

commence	rise	soar	come over
get	mount		

BECOMING *(adjective)*

giving a pleasing appearance or effect.

Optional Words:

attractive	flattering	correct	tasteful
nice	proper	seeming	right
suitable			

BEFIT *(verb)*

to be right and suitable.

Optional Words:

become	suit	fit	agree (with)

BEFORE *(adverb)*

at an earlier time; earlier than; in advance; in readiness; ahead of; in front of.

Optional Words:

ante	fore	previously	beforehand
earlier	formerly		

B

. . . .

BEFRIEND *(verb)*

to become friends with.

Optional Words:

ally	associate	abet	help
assist	foster	sustain	support
uphold			

BEGET *(verb)*

to give rise to; to cause to be.

Optional Words:

bear	breed	generate	multiply
produce	propagate	reproduce	procreate

BEGIN *(verb)*

to come into existence; to arise.

Optional Words:

commence	originate	start	spring from
found	inaugurate	initiate	

BEGUILE *(verb)*

to win the attention or interest of; to amuse.

Optional Words:

charm	finesse	maneuver	play
wile	bemuse		

. . . .

B

BEHAVE *(verb)*

to conduct (oneself) properly or suitably.

Optional Words:

act	bear	comport	conduct

BEHOLD *(verb)*

to see; to observe.

Optional Words:

gaze	glance	scan	survey
view	discern	note	distinguish
notice			

BEHOLDEN *(adjective)*

owing thanks.

Optional Words:

obliged	indebted

BEING *(noun)*

something that exists and has life.

Optional Words:

existence	actuality	entity

B

··

BELIEVE *(verb)*

to accept as true; to have religious faith.

Optional Words:

credit	**trust**	**deem**	**think**
feel			

BELLE *(noun)*

a beautiful woman; a reigning social beauty.

Optional Words:

beauty

BELLOW *(noun)*

a deep shout.

Optional Words:

bluster	**clamor**	**rout**	**roar**
bark			

BELONG *(verb)*

to be rightly assigned; to be a member.

Optional Words:

pertain	**fit**	**suitable**	**appropriate**

···················

B

BELOVED *(adjective)*

dearly loved.

Optional Words:

favorite	precious	truelove	sweetheart
dear	adored	cherished	idolized
prized	revered		

BEND *(verb)*

to turn in a new direction.

Optional Words:

curve	angle	deflect	refract
turn	fold	realign	

BENEDICTION *(noun)*

a spoken blessing; the giving of thanks.

Optional Words:

grace	benison	thanks	approbation

BENEFIT *(noun)*

something helpful, favorable or profitable; also a performance or game held in order to raise money; a fund-raiser.

Optional Words:

advantage	favor	interest	welfare

B

BENIGN *(adjective)*

mild and gentle in its effect.

Optional Words:

charitable	generous	gracious	favorable
helpful	kind	merciful	benevolent

BENISON *(noun)*

a blessing.

Optional Words:

prayer	benediction

BENT *(noun)*

a natural skill or liking.

Optional Words:

bias	leaning	tendency	talent
faculty	flair	genius	knack

BEQUEATH *(verb)*

to leave as a legacy.

Optional Words:

will	leave	transmit	hand down
pass (on)			

• •

BESIDE *(preposition)*

at the side of; close to.

Optional Words:

adjacent   alongside   by   next to

BESOTTED *(adjective)*

infatuated.

Optional Words:

enamored   smitten

BESPEAK *(verb)*

to engage beforehand.

Optional Words:

address   indicate   attest   reserve

solicit   betoken

BEST *(adjective)*

of the most excellent kind.

Optional Words:

optimal   optimum   largest   superlative

utmost   choicest   elite   exemplar

prime   prize   top   paragon

B

BESTOW *(verb)*

to present as a gift.

Optional Words:

confer	donate	give	devote
hand-out			

BETIDE *(verb)*

to happen to.

Optional Words:

befall   occur to

BETOKEN *(verb)*

to be a sign of.

Optional Words:

indicate	promise	testify	witness
announce	attest		

BETROTH *(verb)*

to engage with a promise to marry.

Optional Words:

affiance	intend	pledge	contract

B

• •

BETTER *(adjective)*

of a more excellent kind.

Optional Words:
preferable   superior

(verb)
to improve.

Optional Words:
refine   amend   help

(verb)
surpass.

Optional Words:
exceed

BEVY *(noun)*

a large group.

Optional Words:
assembly	**band**	**bunch**	**cluster**
covey	**crew**	**flock**	

BEWITCH *(verb)*

to put under a magic spell; to delight very much.

Optional Words:
enchant	**possess**	**captivate**	**beguile**
charm	**entice**	**fascinate**	

BEYOND *(preposition)*

at or to the further side of; further on.

Optional Words:
besides	**else**	**farther**	**further**
past			

Defined Words and Options
Page 57
• • • • • • • • • • • • • • • • •

B

BIAS *(noun)*

an opinion, feeling, or influence that strongly favors one side or one item in a group or series.

Optional Words:
**inclination   partiality   preference   slant
angle**

BIBLE *(noun)*

the Christian scriptures; the Jewish scriptures; (common) a book regarded as authoritative.

Optional Words:
**Holy Writ   Sacred Writ   Scripture   Book of Books
Good Book   Word of God**

BICENTENNIAL *(adjective)*

pertaining to 200th anniversary.

Optional Words:
Bicentenary

BID *(noun)*

an offer of a price in order to buy something.

Optional Words:
**proposal   attempt   suggestion   proposition
effort   try**

· ·

BIDDABLE *(adjective)*

willing to obey.

Optional Words:

amenable	docile	obedient	tractable
obliging	pliable		

BIDE *(verb)*

to wait for a good opportunity.

Optional Words:

abide	linger	remain	stick around
tarry	wait		

BIENNIAL *(adjective)*

lasting or living for two years; occurring once in two years.

BIG *(adjective)*

large in size, amount or intensity; important.

Optional Words:

giant	grand	immense	enormous
great	vast	massive	towering
major	vital	sizable	considerable
lavish	liberal	mature	substantial
hefty	husky	generous	notable
lofty			

B

································

BIJOU *(adjective)*
> small and elegant.
>
> *(noun)*
> a jewel or trinket.

BILLOW *(noun)*
> a great wave.
> ***Optional Words:***
> **surge**   **gush**

BIND *(verb)*
> to hold together; to unite.
> ***Optional Words:***
> **secure**   **truss**   **tie**   **fasten**

BLARNEY *(noun)*
> smooth talk that flatters people.
> ***Optional Words:***
> **adulation**   **flattery**   **sweet-talk**

BLAZE *(noun)*

a bright flame or light.

Optional Words:

flame	flare	incandescence

(verb)

to burn brightly.

Optional Words:

sparkle	illuminate	radiate	glow
glare			

BLAZON *(verb)*

to proclaim; to describe or paint.

Optional Words:

enunciate	sound	broadcast	publish
promulgate	advertise	announce	

BLEND *(verb)*

to mingle.

Optional Words:

combine	fuse	merge	harmonize
amalgamate	integrate	meld	compound
unify	mix	symphonize	synthesize

BLESS *(verb)*

to make sacred or holy with the sign of the Cross; to call holy; to ask divine care or protection.

Optional Words:

bestow	dedicate	endow	favor
grace	sanctify		

B

....

BLISS *(noun)*

perfect happiness.

Optional Words:

ecstasy	elation	exhilaration	jubilation
beatitude			

BLOSSOM *(verb)*

to develop and flourish.

Optional Words:

bloom	bud	flower	flush
glow	radiate		

BODE *(verb)*

to be a sign of; to promise.

Optional Words:

predict	foretell	augur	presage
portend			

BOLD *(adjective)*

confident and courageous.

Optional Words:

brave	intrepid	daring	venturesome
game	audacious	valiant	stouthearted
prominent	dashing		

B

BOND *(noun)*

a uniting, binding force.

Optional Words:

tie	adhesion	attachment	cohesion
link	pact	adherence	connection
union	fusion		

BOOM *(verb)*

to have a period of prosperity or rapid economic growth.

Optional Words:

expand	increase	prosper

BOON *(noun)*

a benefit; a good thing.

Optional Words:

favor	gift	blessing	benevolence

BOOST *(verb)*

to increase the strength, value or good reputation of; to promote.

Optional Words:

advance	raise	encourage	support
hike			

B

●●●●●●●●●●●●●●●●●●●●●●●●●●●●

BOUNCE *(verb)*

to spring back.

Optional Words:
rebound　　**recoil**　　　**recover**　　　**ricochet**

BOW *(noun)*

bending of the head or body in greeting to show respect, agreement.

Optional Words:
curtsy　　　**obeisance**

BRACE *(verb)*

to support; to give firmness to.

Optional Words:
bolster　　**fortify**　　　**reinforce**　　**stabilize**
steady　　　**strengthen**

BRACING *(adverb)*

invigorating; stimulating.

Optional Words:
animating　　**exhilarating**　**quickening**　**vitalizing**

BRAIN *(noun)*

an intelligent clever person.

Optional Words:

genius	intellect	mind	intellectual
wit	head		

BRAINSTORM *(noun)*

a sudden bright idea.

Optional Words:

inspiration   eureka

BRAVE *(adjective)*

showing or feeling no fear.

Optional Words:

bold	confident	daring	venturesome
gallant	heroic	intrepid	stouthearted
valiant	game	stalwart	courageous

BRAVO *(noun)*

a cry of 'well done!'

Optional Words:

Good!

B

BRAVURA *(adjective)*

boldly brilliant or ambitious.

Optional Words:
dashing　　　**daring**

BRAWN *(noun)*

muscular strength.

Optional Words:
might　　　**power**　　　**sinew**　　　**firmness**

BREAK *(noun)*

a fair chance.

Optional Words:
opening　　　**shot**　　　**opportunity**

BREAKTHROUGH *(noun)*

a major advance.

Optional Words:
innovation　　**upgrade**

BREEZE *(verb)*

to move in a light manner.

Optional Words:

float	glide	sail	sweep

BRIGHT *(adjective)*

cheerful; quick-witted; clever.

Optional Words:

blazing	brilliant	dazzling	encouraging
glaring	glowing	hopeful	intelligent
intense	luminous	polished	radiant
rich	shining	splendid	resplendent
lively	vivacious		

BRIO *(noun)*

vivacity.

Optional Words:

verve	zing	dash	élan
spirit	esprit	life	animation
oomph	vim		

BRISK *(adjective)*

active; lively; moving quickly.

Optional Words:

energetic	keen	sharp	stimulating
vigorous	agile	nimble	spry

B

BROAD *(adjective)*

large across; wide; full; complete.

Optional Words:

ample	cultivated	liberal	cosmopolitan
immense	unbiased	spacious	open-minded
progressive	experienced		

BUDDY *(noun)*

a friend.

Optional Words:

chum	comrade	intimate	sidekick

BULK *(noun)*

size or magnitude, especially when great; the majority.

Optional Words:

body	mass	quantity	substance
volume			

BUMPER *(adjective)*

unusually large or plentiful.

Optional Words:

brimming	full

C

C

COMPOSITION
COMPREHEND
COMRADE
CONCEIVE
CONCENTRATE
CONCEPT
CONCERN
CONCOCT
CONCORD
CONCRETE
CONCUR
CONDONE
CONDUCT
CONFER
CONFIDENCE
CONFIGURE
CONFIRM
CONFLUENT
CONFORM
CONGRATULATE
CONGREGATE
CONGRUENT
CONJOIN
CONJURE
CONNECT
CONNOISSEUR
CONQUER
CONSCIENCE
CONSCIOUS
CONSECRATE
CONSENT
CONSERVE
CONSIDER
CONSIDERATION
CONSIGN

CONSISTENT
CONSOLE
CONSOLIDATE
CONSONANCE
CONSORT
CONSPICUOUS
CONSTANCY
CONSTITUTE
CONTACT
CONTEMPLATE
CONTEMPORARY
CONTENT
CONTINGENCY
CONTINUE
CONTRACT
CONTRIBUTE
CONTRIVE
CONTROL
CONVENE
CONVENIENT
CONVENTION
CONVENTIONAL
CONVERSANT
CONVERSATION
CONVERSATIONAL-
IST
CONVERT
CONVINCE
CONVIVIAL
CONVOKE
COOL
COOPERATE
COPE
COPIOUS
CORE

CORKER
COROLLARY
CORRECT
CORRESPOND
CORROBORATE
COSMOPOLITAN
COUNSEL
COUNT
COUNTENANCE
COURAGE
COURSE
COURT
COURTEOUS
COVENANT
CRAVE
CRAZE
CREATE
CREATIVE
CREDENTIALS
CREDIBLE
CREDIT
CROON
CRUCIAL
CRUISE
CRYSTALLINE
CUDDLE
CUE
CULMINATE
CULTIVATE
CULTURE
CURIOUS
CURRENT
CUSHY
CUSTOM

CACHET *(noun)*

a distinguishing mark or seal of prestige or commemoration.

Optional Words:

status	stature	rank	position
standing	dignity		

CALL *(verb)*

to utter in a loud voice.

Optional Words:

convene	muster	send for	summon
vociferate	holler	convoke	hail
greet	bid	invite	

CALM *(adjective)*

quiet and still; casual and confident.

Optional Words:

composed	easy	placid	serene
tranquil	collected	poised	relaxed

CAN *(verb)*

know how to; be able to; permitted to.

C

CAPABLE *(adjective)*

having the ability or capacity.

Optional Words:

apt	expert	competent	accomplished
proficient	skillful	able	

CAPACITY *(noun)*

adequate mental power to receive and understand.

Optional Words:

ability	capability	talent	competence
skill	status	might	state
gift	knack	faculty	qualification
bent	caliber		

CAPER *(verb)*

to jump or run about playfully.

Optional Words:

frisk	frolic	gambol	leap
prance	romp	skip	

CAPITAL *(adjective)*

excellent; standing at the head or beginning.

Optional Words:

chief	main	prime	principal
superb			

CAPTIVATE *(verb)*

to capture the fancy of; to charm.

Optional Words:

dazzle	enchant	entrance	fascinate
mesmerize	spellbind	draw	allure
appeal	enamor	magnetize	delight

CARE *(noun)*

watchful regard or attention; heed; protection.

Optional Words:

custody	supervision	guardianship consideration

(verb)

to feel concern, interest, affection or liking.

Optional Words:

love	like	fancy	cherish

CAREFREE *(adjective)*

free from anxiety or responsibility.

Optional Words:

breezy	heedless	nonchalant	optimistic
relaxed	sunny	foot-loose	lithesome

CAREFUL *(adjective)*

done with care.

Optional Words:

circumspect	guarded	meticulous	conscientious
observant	wary	cautious	scrupulous
discreet	safe	mindful	

C

....

CARESS (noun)

a loving touch.

Optional Words:

embrace   massage   hug

CARNIVAL (noun)

festivities and public merrymaking, usually with a procession.

Optional Words:

celebration   circus   fair   gala
jamboree   jubilee   sideshow   event
festival

CAROL (noun)

joyful song, especially a Christmas hymn.

Optional Words:

tune   melody

(verb)
to sing joyfully.

Optional Words:

perform   warble   trill   accompany
sing

CARVE (verb)

to cut with preciseness.

Optional Words:

cleave   dissect   engrave   etch
hew   saw   sculpt   slice
chip

....

C

CATCHWORD *(noun)*

a memorable word or phrase that is often used.

Optional Words:

byword	shibboleth	motto	catch phrase
slogan	maximum		

CATCHY *(adjective)*

pleasant and easy to remember.

Optional Words:

bouncy	infectious	lively	snappy
spirited			

CELEBRATE *(verb)*

to do something to show that a day or event is important; to honor with festivities; to make merry on such an occasion; to officiate at a religious ceremony.

Optional Words:

acclaim	applaud	cheer	commemorate
consecrate	exalt	glorify	hallow
laud	observe	rejoice	ritualize
solemnize	venerate	eulogize	distinguish
regard	revel	recognize	extol
praise	commend	hail	bless
revere			

CELEBRATION *(noun)*

something done in commeration of an event; a festivity.

Optional Words:

carnival	fair	feast	gala
holiday	jamboree	jubilee	party
event	banquet	festival	fiesta

C

CELEBRITY *(noun)*
a well-known person.

Optional Words:

dignitary	luminary	name	notable
star	personality		

(noun)
fame.

Optional Words:

notoriety	popularity	renown	stardom

CELERITY *(noun)*
quickness of motion.

Optional Words:

alacrity	dispatch	swiftness	expedience
haste	speed		

CELESTIAL *(adjective)*
of heaven.

Optional Words:

angelic	astral	glorious	godly
planetary	stellar	sublime	utopian
divine	cosmic		

CENTURY *(noun)*
a period of 100 years.

Optional Words:

centenary	era

CEREMONY *(noun)*

a set of formal acts, especially those used on religious or public occasions.

Optional Words:

liturgy   rite   ritual   service event

(noun)

a formal politeness.

Optional Words:

decorum   etiquette   formality   propriety protocol

CERTAINLY *(adverb)*

with assurance and conviction; yes.

Optional Words:

absolutely   definitely   positively   unquestionably surely

CERTIFICATE *(noun)*

an official written or printed statement.

Optional Words:

affidavit   credential   deed   diploma
document   testimonial   voucher

CHANCE *(noun)*

an opportunity; an occasion when success seems very probable.

Optional Words:

destiny   fate   fortune   likelihood
luck   possibility   probability

C

CHANGE *(verb)*

to make or become different.

Optional Words:

alter	convert	correct	exchange
modify	replace	reverse	vary
shift	substitute	swap	switch
transfigure	transform	vary	

CHARITY *(noun)*

leniency or tolerance; generosity; loving kindness towards others.

Optional Words:

altruism	benefaction	benevolence	compassion
contribution	donation	munificence	

CHARM *(noun)*

attractiveness; the power of arousing love or admiration.

Optional Words:

allure	appeal	charisma	enchantment
fascination	magnetism		

(verb)

to give pleasure to; to influence by personal charm.

Optional Words:

beguile	captivate	delight	entice
enchant	seduce	tempt	

CHAT *(verb)*

to engage in friendly, informal conversation.

Optional Words:

talk	gab	converse	prattle

CHECK *(verb)*

to test or examine in order to make sure that something is correct or in good condition.

Optional Words:

observe	test	examine	try out
corroborate	inspect	study	investigate
validate	verify		

CHEER *(noun)*

a shout of encouragement or applause; cheerfulness.

Optional Words:

animation	fun	gaiety	hooray
joy	merriment	optimism	reassurance
triumph	joviality	happiness	glee
gaiety	merrymaking		

(verb)

to utter a cheer; to encourage or applaud with cheers; to comfort; to gladden.

Optional Words:

brighten	enliven	hearten	inspire
roar	root	yell	amuse
charm	gladden	encourage	enhearten
shout	salute		

CHERISH *(verb)*

to look after lovingly; to be fond of; to keep in one's heart.

Optional Words:

adore	appreciate	esteem	prize
revere	treasure	value	

C

CHERUB *(noun)*

an angelic child.

Optional Words:
angel   **seraph**

CHILDLIKE *(adjective)*

having the good qualities of a child; simplicity and innocence.

Optional Words:

believing	**genuine**	**gullible**	**honest**
ingenuous	**open**	**trusting**	**naive**

CHIRPY *(adjective)*

lively and cheerful.

Optional Words:

happy	**quick**	**gay**	**bright**
lighthearted	**fun**	**spirited**	

CHOOSE *(verb)*

to select out of a greater number of things; to decide; to prefer; to desire.

Optional Words:

adopt	**cull**	**determine**	**discriminate**
distinguish	**elect**	**embrace**	**espouse**
pick	**separate**		

C

CHRIST *(noun)*

The Savior, Jesus, Jesus of Nazareth, the Anointed, the Redeemer, Messiah, Immanuel, the Mediator, the Advocate, the Judge, the Word, the Son, the Son of God, the Risen, Prince of Peace, the Lamb of God, King of Kings, Alpha and Omega, Lord of Lords, the Way, the Light, the Bread of Life, the King of Glory.

CHRISTENING *(noun)*

the ceremony of baptizing or naming.

Optional Words:
sacrament   baptism

CHRISTMAS *(noun)*

the Christian festival commemorating **Christ**'s birth.

Optional Words:
Yuletide   the Nativity   Noel   Christmastide

CHUCKLE *(noun)*

a quiet or half-suppressed laugh.

(verb)
to give a chuckle.

Optional Words:
**chortle   giggle   snicker   laugh
titter**

C

CHUM *(noun)*

a close friend.

Optional Words:

buddy	**comrade**	**intimate**	**sidekick**
associate	**crony**	**companion**	

CINCH *(noun)*

a certainty; an easy task.

Optional Words:

snap	**breeze**	**duck soup**	**picnic**

CIRCLE *(noun)*

a number of people bound together by similar interests.

Optional Words:

circuit	**domain**	**field**	**group**
realm	**ring**	**set**	

CIRCULATE *(verb)*

to go around continuously; to pass from place to place.

Optional Words:

advertise	**circle**	**course**	**disperse**
distribute	**flow**	**issue**	**disseminate**
promote	**publicize**	**travel**	**spread**

C

CIRCUMSTANCE *(noun)*

any of the conditions or facts connected with an event, person or action; ceremony.

Optional Words:

case	estate	formality	happening
incident	pageantry	pomp	occurrence
situation	state		

CIVIL *(adjective)*

polite and obliging.

Optional Words:

civic	cordial	courteous	mannerly
personal	polite		

CIVILIZATION *(noun)*

a stage in the evolution of organized society.

Optional Words:

culture	refinement	sophistication

CLAIM *(verb)*

to declare that something is true or has been achieved.

Optional Words:

affirm	collect	command	demand
exact	maintain	profess	contend
call	warrant	assert	defend
justify			

C

· ·

CLAP *(verb)*

to strike the palms loudly together especially in applause.

Optional Words:

slap	smack	strike	thump

CLARIFY *(verb)*

to make or become clearer or easier to understand.

Optional Words:

define	elucidate	explain	illuminate
simplify	settle	purify	straighten out
cleanse	clean	clearup	

CLASP *(noun)*

a grasp; a handshake.

Optional Words:

bolt	buckle	button	clip

(verb)

to fasten; to join with a clasp; to hold or embrace closely.

Optional Words:

couple	hook	latch	link
lock	secure		

CLASS *(noun)*

a division according to quality.

Optional Words:

category	caste	course	elegance
flair	genre	group	panache
position	refinement	section	seminar
session	sort	station	status
style	variety		

C

CLASSIC *(adjective)*

having a high quality that is recognized and unquestioned; famous through being long established.

Optional Words:

ancient	archetypal	definitive	authoritative
excellent	model	prime	time-honored
superior	typical	masterpiece	well-established

CLEAN *(adjective)*

free from dirt or impurities.

Optional Words:

chaste	decent	decorous	flawless
honorable	immaculate	moral	neat
orderly	perfect	pure	sanitary
spotless	tidy	trim	virtuous
wholesome	bright	fresh	

CLEAR *(adjective)*

transparent; free from blemishes; easily seen, heard or understood; distinct; evident; free from doubt.

Optional Words:

alert	apparent	articulate	bright
crystalline	discerning	intelligible	keen
lucid	obvious	open	translucent

CLEVER *(adjective)*

quick at learning and understanding things.

Optional Words:

adroit	alert	astute	scintillating
bright	dexterous	expert	imaginative
keen	ingenious	handy	inventive
piquant	quick	sharp	resourceful
smart	sparkling	witty	intelligent
skillful			

C

CLIMATE *(noun)*

a general attitude or feeling; an atmosphere.

Optional Words:

ambiance	milieu	mood	surroundings
spirit	environment		

CLIMAX *(noun)*

the event or point of greatest interest or intensity.

Optional Words:

acme	apex	top	culmination
zenith	cap	crown	turning point

CLIMB *(verb)*

to go up or over by effort; to move upwards; to go higher.

Optional Words:

ascend	clamber	escalate	mount
scale			

CLINCH *(verb)*

to settle conclusively.

Optional Words:

assure	cinch	confirm	decide
ensure	secure		

· ·

CLING *(verb)*

to hold on tightly; to become attached; to stick; to remain close or in contact; to be emotionally attached or dependent.

Optional Words:

adhere	be faithful	cherish	clasp
cleave	clench	clutch	grip

CLOSE *(adjective)*

near in space or time; near in relationship.

Optional Words:

akin	attentive	congested	cramped
crowded	dense	devoted	familiar
immediate	imminent	intimate	neighboring
keen	similar		

COAX *(verb)*

to persuade gently or gradually.

Optional Words:

cajole	implore	induce	persuade
urge	sweet-talk	tempt	entice

COEQUAL *(adjective)*

equal to one another.

Optional Words:

even	level	symmetrical

C

COEXISTENCE *(noun)*

mutual tolerance.

Optional Words:
concurrence

COGITATE *(verb)*

to think deeply.

Optional Words:

contemplate	**deliberate**	**meditate**	**ponder**
reflect	**reason**	**speculate**	**cerebrate**

COGNIZANT *(adjective)*

aware; having knowledge.

Optional Words:

conscious	**conversant**	**familiar**	**sensible**
witty	**alive**		

COHERE *(verb)*

to stick together; to remain united in a mass.

Optional Words:

adhere	**agree**	**bond**	**cling**
coincide	**correspond**	**harmonize**	**hold**

COHORT *(noun)*

a companion or follower.

Optional Words:

assistant	colleague	companion	comrade
coworker	friend	partner	associate
confrere	mate	fellow	

COINCIDE *(verb)*

to agree; to be of one opinion, idea or interest.

Optional Words:

concur	conform	correspond	harmonize
assent			

COINCIDENCE *(noun)*

a remarkable occurrence of similar or corresponding events at the same time by chance.

Optional Words:

luck	fluke	fate	concurrence
happenstance			

COLLABORATE *(verb)*

to work in partnership.

Optional Words:

collude	conspire	cooperate	join
unite	help		

C

COLLEAGUE *(noun)*

a fellow member of an official body or profession.

Optional Words:

associate	compatriot	fellow	confrere
partner	comrade	helper	

COLLECT *(verb)*

to bring or come together; to fetch; to gather into systematic order or control.

Optional Words:

accumulate	aggregate	amass	assemble
compile	congregate	convene	gather

COLOSSAL *(adjective)*

immense, remarkable or splendid.

Optional Words:

elephantine	enormous	gigantic	huge
massive	ponderous		

COLOR *(verb)*

to put color on; to paint, stain or dye; to give a special character or bias to.

Optional Words:

hue	cast	shade	tinge
tint			

C

COMBINE *(verb)*

to join or be joined into a group, set or mixture.

Optional Words:

associate	blend	connect	commingle
fuse	link	merge	synthesize
unite	mix	interact	interconnect
wed	fuse	blend	intermingle
merge	pool		

COME *(verb)*

to arrive; to reach a point, condition or result; to take or occupy a specified position.

Optional Words:

advance	appear	approach	enter
extend	happen	spread	show up
reach	get in		

COMEDY *(noun)*

a light, amusing play or film; an amusing incident; humor.

Optional Words:

farce	joking	parody	buffoonery
raillery	satire	wit	funniness
humorousness			

COMELY *(adjective)*

good-looking.

Optional Words:

appealing	attractive	beautiful	decorous
handsome	pretty	proper	seemly
tasteful	bonny	fair	pulchritudinous
lovely			

C

••••••••••••••••••••••••••••••

COMFORT *(noun)*

a state of ease and contentment.

Optional Words:

abundance	luxury	opulence	peace
plenty	serenity	solace	

COMIC *(adjective)*

causing amusement or laughter.

Optional Words:

absurd	droll	farcical	funny
humorous	ludicrous	ridiculous	slapstick
vaudevillian	comical	laughable	hilarious

COMING *(adjective)*

immediately following.

Optional Words:

nearing	next	upcoming

COMITY *(noun)*

courtesy; friendship for mutual benefit.

Optional Words:

goodwill	amity	harmony	benevolence
friendship	kindness	accord	good-fellowship
friendliness	camaraderie		

C

COMMAND *(noun)*

a statement, given with authority, that some action must be performed.

Optional Words:

ability	directive	dominion	expertise
injunction	leadership	mastery	order
rule	skill	power	authority

COMMEMORATE *(verb)*

to keep in the memory by means of a celebration or ceremony.

Optional Words:

acclaim	applaud	cheer	consecrate
exalt	glorify	hallow	honor
laud	observe	rejoice	revel
revere	ritualize	solemnize	venerate

COMMENCE *(verb)*

to begin.

Optional Words:

activate	establish	found	generate
inaugurate	initiate	institute	launch
motivate	originate	start	trigger

COMMEND *(verb)*

to praise; to recommend.

Optional Words:

acclaim	advocate	applaud	approve
compliment	confide	endorse	extol
promote			

C

COMMISSION *(noun)*

the giving of authority to someone to perform a certain task or duty.

Optional Words:

agency	board	committee	council
office			

COMMIT *(verb)*

to pledge; to bind with an obligation.

Optional Words:

dedicate	devote	practice	promise
relegate	swear		

COMMODIOUS *(adjective)*

roomy.

Optional Words:

ample	homelike	spacious	comfortable
suitable	wide		

COMMODITY *(noun)*

an article of trade; a product.

Optional Words:

asset	goods	items	merchandise
stock	vendible	wares	possession
line			

COMMUNICATE *(verb)*

to make known; to transfer; to transmit; to pass news and information to and fro; to succeed in conveying information.

Optional Words:

converse	convey	disclose	correspond
inform	notify	proclaim	reach
talk	write	impart	pass on
transmit			

COMMUNION *(noun)*

fellowship; having ideas or beliefs in common; those that accept each other's doctrines and sacraments; social dealings between people.

Optional Words:

faction	band	regiment	solidarity

COMMUNIQUÉ *(noun)*

an official communication.

Optional Words:

notice	dispatch	report	memorandum
announcement			

COMMUNITY *(noun)*

a body of people living in one place, district or country and considered as a whole; a group with common interests or origins.

Optional Words:

citizenry	population	people	neighborhood
society	public	fellowship	

C

COMPACT *(noun)*

an agreement; a contract.

Optional Words:

alliance	bargain	treaty	confederation
convention	pact	charter	

COMPANION *(noun)*

a person who accompanies another.

Optional Words:

associate	buddy	comrade	fellow
friend	mate		

COMPASSION *(noun)*

showing of pity at the misfortune of others.

Optional Words:

charity	clemency	empathy	commiseration
grace	leniency	pity	sympathy

COMPATIBLE *(adjective)*

capable of living together harmoniously; able to exist or be used together.

Optional Words:

agreeable	appropriate	congruous	fitting
suitable	co-operative		

COMPETENT *(adjective)*

having the ability or authority to do what is required.

Optional Words:

adept	efficient	expert	proficient
qualified	skilled		

COMPETITION *(noun)*

a contest in which people try to do better than the alternative side.

Optional Words:

contention	event	match	tournament
meet	race		

COMPILE *(verb)*

to collect.

Optional Words:

accumulate	amass	assemble	gather
unite	compose		

COMPLACENT *(adjective)*

self-satisfied.

Optional Words:

apathetic	at ease	content	impervious
indifferent	nonchalant		

C

COMPLAISANT *(adjective)*

willing to do what pleases another.

Optional Words:

affable	agreeable	friendly	gracious
indulgent	obliging	pleasant	accommodating
easy	lenient	mild	good-humored
amiable	generous		

COMPLEMENT *(noun)*

that which makes a thing complete.

Optional Words:

accessory	supplement	continuation	supernumerary
extension	reinforcement		

COMPLETE *(adjective)*

having all its parts; not lacking anything; finished; thorough in every way.

Optional Words:

absolute	entire	perfect	comprehensive
radical	thorough	total	unabridged
undivided	whole		

(verb)
to finish.

Optional Words:

achieve	crown	execute	fulfill
terminate			

COMPLIMENT *(noun)*

an expression of praise or admiration either in words or by action.

Optional Words:

adulation	honor	tribute	commendation

COMPLY *(verb)*

to do as one is asked.

Optional Words:

conform	follow	obey	observe
mind	keep		

COMPORT *(verb)*

to behave; to suit; to befit.

Optional Words:

conform	conduct	correspond	harmonize
match			

COMPOSE *(verb)*

to form; to make up; to arrange into good order.

Optional Words:

constitute	create	devise	draft
fashion	form	shape	write

COMPOSITION *(noun)*

a putting together into a whole; an artistic, musical or literary work.

Optional Words:

creation	design	work	constitution
essay	etude	opus	configuration
formation	formulation	invention	construction
paper	piece	theme	

C

COMPREHEND *(verb)*

to grasp mentally; to understand.

Optional Words:

discern	fathom	perceive	accept
catch	cognize	embody	embrace
know			

COMRADE *(noun)*

a companion who shares one's activities.

Optional Words:

ally	associate	colleague	confederate
friend	intimate	pal	partner

CONCEIVE *(verb)*

to form an opinion in the mind; to imagine.

Optional Words:

create	envisage	envision	initiate
invent	make	originate	understand
produce	start	ponder	comprehend
think			

CONCENTRATE *(verb)*

to employ all one's thought, attention or effort on something;
to bring or come together in one place.

Optional Words:

amass	center	cluster	compact
condense	consolidate	converge	fasten
fix	focus	integrate	unify

CONCEPT *(noun)*

an idea; a general notion.

Optional Words:

abstraction	impression	perception	theory
thought	plan		

CONCERN *(verb)*

to be about; to have as its subject; to be of importance to; to affect; to take up the time or attention.

Optional Words:

involve	pertain to	regard

(noun)

something of interest or importance; a responsibility; a connection.

Optional Words:

affair	business	consideration

CONCOCT *(verb)*

to invent.

Optional Words:

beget	build	construct	develop
devise	erect	establish	formulate
generate	institute	make	originate
produce			

CONCORD *(noun)*

agreement or harmony between people or things.

Optional Words:

accord	friendship	goodwill	peace
treaty	unity	harmony	rapport
consonance			

C

....

CONCRETE *(verb)*

to form or set.

Optional Words:

solidify   substantiate

CONCUR *(verb)*

to agree in opinion.

Optional Words:

accede	acquiesce	admit	acknowledge
allow	assent	conform	correspond
fit	harmonize	unite	

CONDONE *(verb)*

to forgive or overlook without punishment.

Optional Words:

approve	disregard	excuse	countenance
ignore	pardon		

CONDUCT *(verb)*

to lead or guide; to manage or direct.

Optional Words:

control	govern	handle	orchestrate

CONFER *(verb)*

to grant or bestow.

Optional Words:

accord	award	bestow	give
grant			

(verb)

to hold a conference or discussion.

Optional Words:

consult	converse	deliberate

CONFIDENCE *(noun)*

a feeling of certainty, self-reliance or boldness.

Optional Words:

aplomb	assurance	belief	self-possession
conviction	faith	poise	determination
surety	purpose		

CONFIGURE *(verb)*

to set up for a particular purpose.

Optional Words:

cast	shape	form	figure

CONFIRM *(verb)*

to provide supporting evidence for the truth or correctness of; to establish more firmly; to make definite or valid formally.

Optional Words:

affirm	authenticate	corroborate	ratify
sanction	settle	substantiate	verify
testify			

C

CONFLUENT *(adjective)*

flowing together.

Optional Words:
gathering   uniting

CONFORM *(verb)*

to keep to rules or general custom.

Optional Words:

adapt	adjust	agree	accommodate
comply	correspond	follow	harmonize
obey	observe		

CONGRATULATE *(verb)*

to praise and tell that one is pleased about another's achievement or good fortune.

Optional Words:
applaud   compliment   felicitate   hail

CONGREGATE *(verb)*

to flock together.

Optional Words:

amass	assemble	collect	gather
throng	group	converge	

C

CONGRUENT *(adjective)*

suitably consistent; having exactly the same shape and size.

Optional Words:

comparable	compatible	fitting	complementary
congruous	proper	similar	corresponding
harmonious	suitable		

CONJOIN *(verb)*

to join together.

Optional Words:

adhere	adjoin	affix	associate
attach	combine	connect	consolidate
enlist	enroll	enter	fasten
fuse	meet	merge	secure
splice	syndicate	unite	wed
yoke	couple		

CONJURE *(verb)*

to call or appeal solemnly; to produce in the mind.

Optional Words:

invoke	summon	evoke

CONNECT *(verb)*

to join or be joined.

Optional Words:

associate	attach	bridge	combine
compare	correlate	couple	join
link	relate	span	unite

C

CONNOISSEUR *(noun)*

a person qualified in matters of taste and appreciation.

Optional Words:

aesthete   authority   epicure   expert
gourmet   judge

CONQUER *(verb)*

to win; to overcome by effort.

Optional Words:

master   subdue   surmount   triumph over

CONSCIENCE *(noun)*

a person's sense of right and wrong, especially in his or her own actions or motives.

Optional Words:

ethics   morals   principles   scruples
standards   integrity

CONSCIOUS *(adjective)*

with one's mental faculties awake; aware of one's surroundings.

Optional Words:

alert   cognizant   discerning   sensible
sentient

CONSECRATE *(verb)*

to make or declare sacred.

Optional Words:

bless	hallow	sanctify	apotheosize
canonize	dedicate		

CONSENT *(noun)*

agreement to what someone wishes.

Optional Words:

agreement	approval	authorization	acquiescence
concurrence	permission		

CONSERVE *(verb)*

to keep for future use.

Optional Words:

keep	maintain	preserve	reserve
save	protect		

CONSIDER *(verb)*

to think about in order to make a decision.

Optional Words:

appraise	contemplate	deem	deliberate
estimate	figure	judge	ponder
regard	weigh		

C

CONSIDERATION *(noun)*

careful thought; kindness.

Optional Words:

attention	cause	courtesy	factor
interest	meditation	payment	thoughtfulness
point	reflection	regard	respect
tact	thought		

CONSIGN *(verb)*

to hand over or deliver formally; to give into someone's care.

Optional Words:

commit	convey	delegate	entrust
remit	transfer		

CONSISTENT *(adjective)*

conforming to a regular pattern or style.

Optional Words:

agreeable	compatible	congruous	consonant
constant	dependable	invariable	complimentary
steady	unified		

CONSOLE *(verb)*

to comfort.

Optional Words:

calm	cheer	solace	soothe
succor	upraise	hearten	inspirit

CONSOLIDATE *(verb)*

to make or become secure and strong; to combine or become combined; to merge.

Optional Words:

compress	concentrate	condense	incorporate
merge	streamline	unite	

CONSONANCE *(noun)*

agreement.

Optional Words:

accord	harmony	concord	concordance

CONSORT *(verb)*

to associate with; to keep company with.

Optional Words:

associate	fraternize	mingle	socialize

CONSPICUOUS *(adjective)*

easily seen; attracting attention; worthy of notice.

Optional Words:

apparent	evident	marked	distinguished
noticeable	obvious	outstanding	prominent
remarkable	pointed	striking	clear
distinct			

C

CONSTANCY *(noun)*

the quality of being constant and unchanging; faithfulness.

Optional Words:

allegiance	consistency	continuity	devotion
fidelity	loyalty	reliability	uniformity

CONSTITUTE *(verb)*

to make up; to form; to appoint; to establish or be.

Optional Words:

comprise	form	make up	organize
start	establish	create	

CONTACT *(noun)*

touching; coming together; being in touch; communication.

Optional Words:

connection	meeting	nearness	proximity
touch	union	accord	rapport

CONTEMPLATE *(verb)*

to gaze at thoughtfully; to consider; to meditate.

Optional Words:

cogitate	envision	examine	expect
inspect	meditate	picture	ponder
regard	ruminate	see	speculate
study	survey	think	think about
muse			

CONTEMPORARY (adjective)

up to date.

Optional Words:

concurrent   current   fashionable   mod
modern   newfangled   in vogue

CONTENT (adjective)

satisfied with what one has.

Optional Words:

appeased   comfortable   complacent   pleased

CONTINGENCY (noun)

something unforeseen; a possibility; something that may occur at a future date.

Optional Words:

eventuality   likelihood   possibility   potentiality
surprise

CONTINUE (verb)

to keep up; to remain in a certain place or condition; to go further; to begin again.

Optional Words:

abide	carry on	extend	last
persevere	persist	proceed	reach
remain	renew	restart	recommence
resume	stay	run on	endure

C

CONTRACT *(noun)*

a formal agreement between people, groups or countries;
a document setting out the terms of such an agreement.

Optional Words:

agreement	bargain	compact	arrangement
covenant	deal	pact	pledge

CONTRIBUTE *(verb)*

to give jointly with others, especially to a common fund.

Optional Words:

augment	advance	bestow	confer
donate	endow	give	present

CONTRIVE *(verb)*

to plan cleverly; to achieve in a clever or resourceful way.

Optional Words:

concoct	conspire	devise	fashion
improvise	invent	originate	plot
scheme			

CONTROL *(noun)*

the power to give orders; to restrain something.

Optional Words:

authority	command	composure	dominion
jurisdiction	monopoly	power	self-control
sway			

CONVENE *(verb)*

to assemble.

Optional Words:

accumulate	amass	build	collect
compile	congregate	converge	gather
rally			

CONVENIENT *(adjective)*

easy to use or deal with; available or occurring at a suitable time or place.

Optional Words:

accessible	helpful	nearby	advantageous
available	beneficial	handy	

CONVENTION *(noun)*

a formal assembly; a custom.

Optional Words:

agreement	compact	conclave	conference
formality	transaction	precept	understanding
bond	concord	pact	

CONVENTIONAL *(adjective)*

done according to convention.

Optional Words:

common	customary	orthodox	pedestrian
prosaic	regular	standard	traditional

C

CONVERSANT *(adjective)*

having a knowledge of.

Optional Words:

acquainted	familiar	versed in	knowledgeable
aware	well informed		

CONVERSATION *(noun)*

talk between people.

Optional Words:

chat	dialogue	discourse	discussion
talk	tête-à-tête		

CONVERSATIONALIST *(noun)*

a person who is good at conversation.

Optional Words:

talker	speaker	raconteur

CONVERT *(verb)*

to change from one substance, form or use to another.

Optional Words:

alter	change	modify	transform

CONVINCE *(verb)*

to make a person agree or believe by means of an argument or proposition backed by evidence.

Optional Words:

assure	induce	influence	persuade
reassure	satisfy	sway	

CONVIVIAL *(adjective)*

sociable and lively.

Optional Words:

affable	festive	friendly	genial
hearty	jovial	merry	

CONVOKE *(verb)*

to summon; to assemble.

Optional Words:

call	convene	collect	congregate

COOL *(adjective)*

calm and in control.

Optional Words:

bracing	calm	casual	confident
collected	composed	deliberate	fresh
reserved			

C

···························

COOPERATE *(verb)*

to work with another or others.

Optional Words:

collaborate   collude   conspire   participate

COPE *(verb)*

to manage successfully; to deal with successfully.

Optional Words:

contend   endure   handle   manage
survive

COPIOUS *(adjective)*

existing in large amounts.

Optional Words:

abundant   ample   bountiful   generous
profuse

CORE *(noun)*

the central or most important part of something.

Optional Words:

center   crux   essence   gist
heart   middle   nucleus   pith

C

• •

CORKER *(slang)*

an excellent person or thing.

Optional Words:

crackerjack	lulu	dilly	dandy
knockout	jim-dandy	humdinger	

COROLLARY *(noun)*

a natural consequence or result; something that follows logically after something else is proved.

Optional Words:

result	effect	conclusion

CORRECT *(adjective)*

true, accurate or proper; in accordance with an approved way of behaving or working.

Optional Words:

accurate	appropriate	apt	authentic
exact	faithful	fitting	literal
precise	proper	suitable	

CORRESPOND *(verb)*

to be in harmony or agreement.

Optional Words:

agree	coincide	compare	concur
conform	fit	match	

C

CORROBORATE *(verb)*

to get or give supporting evidence.

Optional Words:

confirm	document	support	authenticate
validate	verify		

COSMOPOLITAN *(adjective)*

of or from many parts of the world.

Optional Words:

cultivated	cultured	global	international
urbane	polished	civilized	sophisticated

COUNSEL *(noun)*

advice or suggestions.

Optional Words:

advice	direction	guidance	recommendation
instruction	suggestion		

COUNT *(verb)*

to include or be included in a reckoning; to be important; to be worth reckoning.

Optional Words:

deem	include	involve	judge
matter	mean	number	regard
signify	total		

C

COUNTENANCE *(noun)*

an appearance of approval.

Optional Words:

air	approval	aspect	endorsement
expression	sanction	support	

COURAGE *(noun)*

the ability to control fear and carry on when facing danger or pain.

Optional Words:

boldness	bravery	spirit	determination
endurance	fortitude	nerve	pluck
tenacity	valor	spunk	

COURSE *(noun)*

an onward movement in space or time; the direction taken or intended; a series of things one can do to achieve something.

Optional Words:

action	direction	duration	development
passage	path	policy	progression
route	sequence	span	term
track			

COURT *(verb)*

to try to win the affection of.

Optional Words:

captivate	pursue	spark	allure
attract			

C

COURTEOUS *(adjective)*

characterized by good manners.

Optional Words:

civil	cultivated	gracious	mannerly
polite	refined		

COVENANT *(noun)*

a formal agreement; a contract.

Optional Words:

agreement	bond	contract	arrangement
oath	pact	pledge	promise
treaty	vow	word	understanding

CRAVE *(verb)*

to long for; to have a strong desire.

Optional Words:

covet	desire	hope for	hunger
long for	thirst		

CRAZE *(noun)*

a great but often short lived enthusiasm for something.

Optional Words:

fad	fashion	rage	vogue

CREATE *(verb)*

to bring into existence; to originate.

Optional Words:

beget	build	concoct	construct
develop	devise	erect	establish
formulate	found	generate	institute
invent	make	originate	produce

CREATIVE *(adjective)*

having the ability to create.

Optional Words:

ingenious	innovative	inventive	constructive
novel	fruitful	formative	inceptive
incipient			

CREDENTIALS *(noun)*

documents showing a person's right to perform certain acts.

Optional Words:

certificate	degree	document	license

CREDIBLE *(adjective)*

manifesting reasonable grounds to be believed.

Optional Words:

believable	tenable	dependable	honorable
plausible	probable	reliable	conceivable
solid	sound	straight	trustworthy
convincing			

C

CREDIT *(noun)*

honor or acknowledgment given for some achievement or good quality.

Optional Words:
acclaim   honor   allowance   acknowledgment recognition

CROON *(verb)*

to sing softly and gently.

Optional Words:
carol   chant   intone   lilt serenade   vocalize

CRUCIAL *(adjective)*

very important; deciding an important issue.

Optional Words:
critical   decisive   determining   important significant

CRUISE *(verb)*

to sail about for pleasure.

Optional Words:
float   boat   glide   navigate

(slang)
to drive at moderate speed.

C

CRYSTALLINE *(adjective)*

very clear, like crystal.

Optional Words:

lucent	lucid	pellucid	translucent
clear	transparent		

CUDDLE *(verb)*

to hold closely and lovingly in one's arms.

Optional Words:

fondle	nestle	nuzzle	snuggle
caress	hug		

(noun)

an affectionate hug.

Optional Words:

caress   hug

CUE *(noun)*

something said or done which serves as a signal for something else to be said or done.

Optional Words:

hint	innuendo	lead	suggestion
prompt	sign	signal	

CULMINATE *(verb)*

to reach its highest point or degree.

Optional Words:

cap	climax	complete	conclude
crown	end	finish	consummate
fulfill	top		

C

CULTIVATE (verb)

to spend time and care in developing (a thing); to try to win someone's goodwill.

Optional Words:

court	develop	encourage	enhance
enrich	foster	improve	nourish

CULTURE (noun)

the appreciation and understanding of literature, arts, music, etc.; the customs and civilization of a particular people or group; improvement by care and training.

Optional Words:

breeding	civilization	cultivation	enlightenment
enrichment	erudition	gentility	learning
manners	polish	society	sophistication
class	urbanity		

CURIOUS (adjective)

eager to learn or know about something.

Optional Words:

inquiring	inquisitive	questioning	investigative
searching			

CURRENT (adjective)

belonging to the present time; happening now.

Optional Words:

present	contemporary

. . . .

CUSHY *(slang)*

pleasant and easy.

Optional Words:

comfy	cozy	easeful	soft

CUSTOM *(noun)*

the usual practice of a group; a usual way of behaving or doing something.

Optional Words:

ceremony	convention	duty	etiquette
habit	levy	mode	mores
practice	rite	ritual	tradition

. . . .

D

D

Section Index

DAINTY
DANCE
DARE
DARLING
DASH
DAUNTLESS
DAWN
DAYDREAM
DAYLIGHT
DAZZLE
DEAL
DEAR
DEBUT
DECENT
DECIDE
DECK
DECLARE
DECORATE
DECORUM
DEDICATE
DEED
DEEM
DEFEND
DEFERENCE
DEFINE
DEFT
DELECTABLE
DELEGATE

DELICATE
DELICIOUS
DELIGHT
DELINEATE
DELIRIOUS
DEMONSTRATE
DENOTE
DEPEND
DERIVE
DESCRIBE
DESIGN
DESIGNATE
DESIGNER
DESIRE
DESTINY
DETERMINE
DEVELOP
DEVISE
DEVOTE
DEVOTED
DIADEM
DICTATE
DICTUM
DIGNIFY
DIGNITARY
DIGNITY
DIPLOMACY
DIRECT

DISCIPLE
DISCIPLINE
DISCOVER
DISCRETION
DISPLAY
DISTINCT
DISTINGUISHED
DIVE
DIVERSE
DIVIDEND
DOCUMENT
DOER
DOMESTIC
DONATION
DOTE
DOUBLE
DOVE
DOVETAIL
DRAMATIC
DRAW
DREAM
DRESSY
DRIVE
DUPLICATE
DUTY
DYNAMIC
DYNAMO

D

D

DAINTY *(adjective)*

small and pretty; delicate.

Optional Words:

delectable	delicious	exquisite	fine
tiny	fragile	graceful	particular
petite	refined		

DANCE *(verb)*

to move with rhythmical steps or movements, usually to music.

Optional Words:

cavort	frolic	gambol	jump
perform	skip		

DARE *(verb)*

to have the courage to do something; to be bold; to take the risk; to challenge.

Optional Words:

chance	risk	try	venture

DARLING *(noun)*

a dearly loved or lovable person or thing; a favorite.

Optional Words:

dear	honey	love	pet
sweetheart			

D

....

DASH *(verb)*

to run rapidly; to rush.
Optional Words:
hurry   **speed**   **zip**

DAUNTLESS *(adjective)*

brave; intrepid.
Optional Words:

bold	**confident**	**courageous**	**daring**
fearless	**gallant**	**game**	**stouthearted**
heroic	**valiant**	**stalwart**	

DAWN *(noun)*

the first light of day; the beginning.
Optional Words:

daybreak	**daylight**	**inception**	**morning**
sunrise			

(verb)
to begin to appear or become evident.
Optional Words:

commence	**emerge**	**arise**	**unfold**

DAYDREAM *(noun)*

idle and pleasant thoughts.
Optional Words:

fancy	**fantasy**	**reverie**	**whim**

D

DAYLIGHT *(noun)*

the light of day, dawn; understanding or knowledge.

Optional Words:
morning   sunup

DAZZLE *(verb)*

to amaze and impress by a splendid display.

Optional Words:

amaze	astound	awe	daze
impress	overwhelm		

DEAL *(verb)*

to distribute among several people; to hand out.

Optional Words:

administer	agreement	allot	arrangement
apportion	disperse		

(verb)
to do business with; to take action about.

Optional Words:

bargain	barter	handle	trade

(noun)
a business transaction.

Optional Words:

agreement	arrangement	contract

D

DEAR *(adjective)*

much loved; cherished; esteemed.

Optional Words:
beloved   darling   favorite   precious

(adjective)
expensive.

Optional Words:
costly

(interjection)
an exclamation of surprise.

DEBUT *(noun)*

a first public appearance.

Optional Words:
inauguration

(noun)
the beginning of an action.

Optional Words:
commencement   opening

D

. . . .

DECENT *(adjective)*

characterized by propriety of conduct, speech, manner, or dress; respectable.

Optional Words:
courteous   **gracious**   **proper**   **honorable**

(adjective)
good, kind and generous.

Optional Words:
nice   **obliging**

(adjective)
adequate.

Optional Words:
ample   **acceptable**   **satisfactory**   **sufficient**
suitable   **moderate**   **modest**   **chaste**

DECIDE *(verb)*

to make a choice or judgment; to come to a decision.

Optional Words:
choose   **determine**   **resolve**   **select**

(verb)
to settle by giving victory to one side.

Optional Words:
decree   **elect**   **find**   **judge**
rule   **vote for**

DECK *(verb)*

to decorate; to dress up.

Optional Words:
adorn   **dress**   **festoon**   **ornament**
trim

. . . .

D

DECLARE *(verb)*

to make known or announce openly, formally or explicitly.

Optional Words:

assert	certify	claim	acknowledge
proclaim	pronounce	testify	expound
report	reveal	state	tell

DECORATE *(verb)*

to make more attractive, striking or festive by adding something beautiful.

Optional Words:

adorn	beautify	deck	embellish
enhance	garnish	ornament	trim

(verb)

to confer a medal or other award upon.

Optional Words:
award

DECORUM *(noun)*

correctness and dignity of behavior or procedure.

Optional Words:

breeding	etiquette	gentility	propriety
protocol			

D

DEDICATE *(verb)*

to devote to a sacred person or use.

Optional Words:

bestow   **bless**   **consecrate**   **sanctify**

(verb)

to set apart for a special purpose.

Optional Words:

commit   **donate**   **give**   **pledge**

DEED *(noun)*

something done; an act or action.

Optional Words:

accomplishment   **achievement**

DEEM *(verb)*

to believe; to consider; to judge.

Optional Words:

view   **realize**   **regard**

DEFEND *(verb)*

to protect and keep safe.

Optional Words:

fortify   **guard**   **shield**   **secure**
harbor   **preserve**

D

DEFERENCE *(noun)*

compliance with another person's wishes.

Optional Words:
courtesy   allegiance   consideration

DEFINE *(verb)*

to give the exact meaning of; to state or explain the basic qualities of.

Optional Words:
clarify   delineate   describe   designate
interpret   specify

(verb)
to mark the outline or boundary of.

DEFT *(adjective)*

skillful; quick and neat.

Optional Words:
able   adroit   dexterous   expert

DELECTABLE *(adjective)*

pleasing; charming; enjoyable.

Optional Words:
appetizing   delicious   delightful   gratifying
luscious   savory   lovely   choice
heavenly   ambrosial   scrumptious

D

DELEGATE *(verb)*

to entrust a task, power or responsibility to an agent; to appoint or send as a representative.

Optional Words:

assign   authorize   charge   commission
designate

DELICATE *(adjective)*

pleasing to the senses, especially in a subtle manner.

Optional Words:

delectable   luscious   luxurious   ethereal

(adjective)
of exquisite quality of workmanship.

Optional Words:

refined   excellent   superior

(adjective)
easily damaged.

Optional Words:

dainty   fragile   slight   frail

DELICIOUS *(adjective)*

delightful, especially to the senses of taste or smell.

Optional Words:

appetizing   delectable   luscious   mouthwatering
palatable   savory   scrumptious

D

• •

DELIGHT *(verb)*

to please greatly; to feel great pleasure.

Optional Words:

amuse	charm	cheer	enthrall
gladden	enjoy		

(noun)

great pleasure or enjoyment.

Optional Words:

charm	cheer	joy	enchantment
gratification			

DELINEATE *(verb)*

to show by drawing or describing.

Optional Words:

define	depict	draft	outline
picture	portray	render	sketch
represent	etch		

DELIRIOUS *(adjective)*

wildly excited.

Optional Words:

ecstatic	excited	thrilled	rapturous

DEMONSTRATE *(verb)*

to show evidence of; to prove; to describe and explain by the help of specimens or examples.

Optional Words:

confirm	display	establish	exhibit
illustrate	manifest	evince	

• • • • • • • • • • • • • • •

D

DENOTE *(verb)*

to be the sign, symbol or name of.

Optional Words:

designate   **represent**   **symbolize**   **signify**

DEPEND *(verb)*

to rely on; to trust confidently; to feel certain about.

Optional Words:

bank on   **count on**

DERIVE *(verb)*

to obtain from a source.

Optional Words:

gain	**glean**	**secure**	**acquire**
gather	**extract**	**get**	**procure**

DESCRIBE *(verb)*

to set forth in words or speech.

Optional Words:

delineate	**depict**	**narrate**	**picture**
portray	**recount**	**report**	**express**

(verb)

to characterize something.

Optional Words:

name   **designate**   **specify**

D

DESIGN *(noun)*

a combination of lines or shapes to form a decoration.

Optional Words:

blueprint	composition	motif	pattern
outline	creation	invention	layout

(noun)

a mental plan.

Optional Words:

intention	strategy	scheme

DESIGNATE *(verb)*

to mark or point out clearly; to specify.

Optional Words:

appoint	denote	indicate	label
name	signify	earmark	stipulate

DESIGNER *(noun)*

one who designs things.

Optional Words:

artist	craftsman

DESIRE *(noun)*

an expressed wish.

Optional Words:

ambition	appetite	aspiration	craving
longing	passion	want	yearning
fancy			

D

DESTINY *(noun)*

the fate that a person or thing is destined for; determined in advance.

Optional Words:

fortune	future	karma	kismet
lot	portion		

DETERMINE *(verb)*

to find out or calculate precisely.

Optional Words:

ascertain	define	demarcate	circumscribe
discover	divine	learn	establish
prove	show		

(verb)

to settle; to decide; to be the decisive factor or influence.

Optional Words:

conclude	govern	judge	resolve

DEVELOP *(verb)*

to make or become larger, fuller, more mature or organized.

Optional Words:

amplify	breed	cultivate	enlarge
evolve	extend	generate	incur
produce	ripen	stretch	unfold
realize			

D

DEVISE *(verb)*

> to think out; to plan; to invent.
>
> ***Optional Words:***
> conceive   design   formulate

DEVOTE *(verb)*

> to give or use for a particular activity or purpose.
>
> ***Optional Words:***
> apply   commit   consecrate   consign
> dedicate   pledge   present

DEVOTED *(adjective)*

> feeling or showing strong affection or attachment.
>
> ***Optional Words:***
> faithful   loyal   ardent   staunch
> steadfast   loving   veracious   caring
> attentive   solicitous   zealous   committed

> *(adjective)*
> having been dedicated.
>
> ***Optional Words:***
> hallowed   pledged   confirmed   sanctified
> declared   promised   bound   consecrated

DIADEM *(noun)*

> a crown or headband worn as a sign of sovereignty.
>
> ***Optional Words:***
> coronet   tiara

D

DICTATE *(verb)*

to state or order with authority.

Optional Words:

decree	govern	ordain	prescribe
impose			

DICTUM *(noun)*

a formal expression of opinion; a saying.

Optional Words:

adage	decree	maxim	order
proverb	saying	aphorism	pronouncement
precept	truism		

DIGNIFY *(verb)*

to give dignity to.

Optional Words:

exalt	glorify	honor	raise
aggrandize			

DIGNITARY *(noun)*

one having official position, especially in church or government.

Optional Words:

celebrity	chief	eminence	leader
luminary	VIP		

D

· ·

DIGNITY *(noun)*

showing suitable formality or indicating that one deserves respect.

Optional Words:

cachet	decorum	nobleness	grace
poise	virtue		

(noun)

a high rank or position.

Optional Words:

status	position	prestige	standing

DIPLOMACY *(noun)*

skill and tack in the handling of international relations or in dealing with people.

Optional Words:

delicacy	savoir-faire	poise	tactfulness

DIRECT *(adjective)*

straightforward and frank; going straight to the point.

Optional Words:

candid	explicit	immediate	continuous
exact	complete		

DISCIPLE *(noun)*

any of the original followers of **Christ**; a person who follows the teachings of another whom he or she accepts as a leader.

Optional Words:

apostle	believer	devotee	pupil
convert			

D

DISCIPLINE *(noun)*

training that produces obedience, self-control or a particular skill.

Optional Words:

branch	training	method	concentration
order	regimen	specialty	indoctrination

DISCOVER *(verb)*

to obtain sight or knowledge of, especially by searching or other effort; to be the first to do this.

Optional Words:

ascertain	detect	determine	find
learn	locate	realize	understand
recognize			

DISCRETION *(noun)*

good judgment; freedom or authority to act according to one's judgment.

Optional Words:

caution	prudence	sense	wisdom

DISPLAY *(verb)*

to show; to arrange (a thing) for exhibition.

Optional Words:

exhibit	parade	represent	demonstrate

D

· ·

DISTINCT *(adjective)*

able to be perceived clearly by the senses or the mind; definite and unmistakable.

Optional Words:

apparent	clear	dissimilar	distinctive
intelligible	lucid	particular	plain
separate	sharp	special	well-defined

DISTINGUISHED *(adjective)*

showing excellence; famous for great achievements.

Optional Words:

celebrated	dignified	elegant	famous
grand	great	notable	refined

DIVE *(verb)*

to plunge head first into something.

Optional Words:

fall	jump	plummet	plunge

DIVERSE *(adjective)*

of different kinds.

Optional Words:

assorted	different	distinct	eclectic
sundry	various		

· · · · · · · · · · · · · · · · ·

D

DIVIDEND *(noun)*

a benefit from an action.

Optional Words:
bonus　　**perquisite**　**premium**　　**profit**

(noun)

a quantity divided into equal parts.

Optional Words:
percentage　**portion**　　**share**

DOCUMENT *(verb)*

to prove or provide evidence.

Optional Words:
certify　　　**substantiate**　**support**

DOER *(noun)*

a person who does something; one who takes action.

Optional Words:
mover　　　**operator**　　**promoter**　　**performer**
worker

DOMESTIC *(adjective)*

of the home, household or family affairs.

Optional Words:
household　**indigenous**　**native**

D

DONATION *(noun)*

an act of donating; a gift of money, etc. to a fund or institution.

Optional Words:

aid	assistance	bestowal	charity
contribution	endowment	gift	grant
gratuity	offering	presentation	benefaction

DOTE *(verb)*

to show great fondness.

Optional Words:

baby	coddle	humor	indulge
spoil	idolize	adore	worship

DOUBLE *(adjective)*

combining two things or qualities.

Optional Words:

coupled	paired	twice	twined
two-fold	bifold	binary	dual
dualistic	duplex		

DOVE *(noun)*

a person who favors a policy of peace and negotiations rather than violence.

Optional Words:

pacifist	peacemaker

D

DOVETAIL (verb)

to join or fit closely together; to combine neatly.

Optional Words:

agree	accord	correspond	fit (in)
harmonize	jibe	square	tally

DRAMATIC (adjective)

exciting; impressive.

Optional Words:

sensational	spectacular	striking	theatrical

DRAW (verb)

to attract; to take in; to get information from.

Optional Words:

deduce	derive	entice	evoke
select			

DREAM (noun)

an ambition or ideal; a beautiful person or thing.

Optional Words:

aspiration	desire	goal	hope
vision	wish		

D

DRESSY *(adjective)*

wearing stylish clothes; elegant; elaborate.

Optional Words:
fashionable   classy   embellished   decorative

DRIVE *(verb)*

to keep going; to cause; to rush; to move or be moved rapidly.

Optional Words:

motivate	**pilot**	**press**	**propel**
steer	**urge**	**actuate**	**impel**
propel	**mobilize**		

DUPLICATE *(noun)*

one of two or more things that are exactly alike; an exact copy.

Optional Words:

counterpart	**double**	**imitation**	**match**
replica	**twin**	**mirror**	**reproduction**

DUTY *(noun)*

a moral or legal obligation; a task that must be done; action required from a particular person.

Optional Words:

assignment	**charge**	**function**	**responsibility**
obligation	**office**		

D

DYNAMIC *(adjective)*

of or relating to motion; energetic; having force of character.

Optional Words:

active	appealing	charismatic	forceful
magnetic	powerful	vibrant	vigorous
vital	lusty	intense	vehement
masterful	alive	exciting	puissant
omnipotent	explosive	impressive	thrilling
dramatic	zealous	spirited	exuberant
robust	peppy	fervent	sensational

DYNAMO *(noun)*

a person or thing with great vitality or effectiveness.

Optional Words:

activist	magnet	master	enthusiast

E

E

E

EXTEND
EXTOL
EXTRA
EXTRAVAGANZA
EXTREME
EXTROVERT
EXUBERANT
EXULT
EYE-OPENER

E

EAGER *(adjective)*

full of strong desire; enthusiastic.

Optional Words:

avid	earnest	excited	enthusiastic
zealous	agog	keen	raring
gung ho	ambitious	intent	

EARN *(verb)*

to get or deserve a reward for one's work or merit.

Optional Words:

acquire	collect	draw	gain
net	obtain	reap	secure
warrant	win		

EARNEST *(adjective)*

showing sincere feeling or intentions.

Optional Words:

devoted	diligent	enthusiastic	heartfelt
intent	solemn	thoughtful	

EASE *(verb)*

to free from discomfort, worry or pain.

Optional Words:

soothe	calm	alleviate	relieve

(verb)
to move gently or gradually.

E

....

EDIFY (verb)

to instruct, especially so as to be an uplifting influence on the mind.

Optional Words:

direct	enlighten	guide	improve
illuminate	irradiate	enhance	better

EFFECT (noun)

a change produced by an action or cause; a result; an impression produced on a spectator.

Optional Words:

aftermath	conclusion	impact	consequence
outcome			

EFFICACIOUS (adjective)

producing or able to produce an intended effect.

Optional Words:

efficient	effectual	skillful	adroit
expert			

ELATE (verb)

to cause to feel very pleased or proud; to raise the spirits of.

Optional Words:

cheer	delight	exhilarate	please
thrill	overjoy	gladden	buoy
commove	inspire	stimulate	exalt
elevate	excite		

ELECT *(verb)*

to choose by vote; to choose as a course.

Optional Words:

determine	resolve	select	settle
vote	decide		

ELECTRIC *(adjective)*

thrilling.

Optional Words:

charged	exciting	lively	electrifying
spirited	magnetic	thrilling	

ELECTRIFY *(verb)*

to charge with electricity; to excite suddenly.

Optional Words:

astonish	energize	rouse	stir
thrill	enthuse	instill	

ELEGANT *(adjective)*

tasteful, refined and dignified in appearance or style.

Optional Words:

charming	cultivated	debonair	exquisite
graceful	gracious	ornate	sophisticated
suave	tasteful		

E

ELEVATE *(verb)*

to raise to a higher place or position.

Optional Words:

heave	heighten	hoist	levitate
lift			

(verb)

to raise to a higher moral or intellectual level.

Optional Words:

heighten   exalt   ennoble

ELIGIBLE *(adjective)*

qualified to be chosen for a position or allowed a privilege; regarded as suitable or desirable.

Optional Words:

acceptable	available	fit	qualified
worthy	likely	suited	

ELITE *(noun)*

a group of people regarded as superior and therefore favored.

Optional Words:

aristocracy	celebrities	cream	gentry
nobility	select	society	gentility
upper crust	cre'me de la cre'me		

ELOQUENCE *(noun)*

fluent, persuasive and powerful speaking.

Optional Words:

style   effectiveness   persuasiveness

EMANCIPATE *(verb)*

to liberate; to set free.

Optional Words:

release   free   loose

EMBARK *(verb)*

to begin an undertaking.

Optional Words:

commence   launch   set sail   start

EMBELLISH *(verb)*

to ornament; to improve by adding details.

Optional Words:

adorn	color	decorate	dress up
elaborate	beautify	emblaze	enrich
deck	bedeck		

E

....

EMBRACE *(verb)*

to hold closely and affectionately in one's arms.

Optional Words:

clasp	hug	squeeze	grip
cling	hold	cradle	

(verb)

to accept eagerly.

Optional Words:

encircle	fold	adopt

(verb)

to include.

Optional Words:

adopt	comprise	contain	encompass
incorporate	encircle	fold	

EMERGE *(verb)*

to come into view.

Optional Words:

appear	arise	dawn	loom
materialize	show	spring	surface

EMIT *(verb)*

to send out matter or energy; to utter.

Optional Words:

beam	broadcast	discharge	give off
issue	transmit	radiate	

E

EMOTION *(noun)*

an intense mental feeling.

Optional Words:
**passion   sensation   sentiment   responsiveness
feeling   affection**

EMPATHY *(noun)*

the ability to identify oneself mentally with a person or thing.

Optional Words:
**comfort   compassion   sensitivity   understanding
solace   feeling**

EMPHASIS *(noun)*

special importance given to something.

Optional Words:
prominence   consideration   significance

(noun)
vigor of expression, feeling or action.

Optional Words:
force

(noun)
the extra force used in speaking a particular syllable or word.

Optional Words:
accent   stress

E

∙ ∙

EMPIRE *(noun)*

supreme power.

Optional Words:

domain	kingdom	nation	commonwealth
ruler	state	sovereignty	

EMPOWER *(verb)*

to give power or authority to.

Optional Words:

authorize	commission	entrust	license
warrant	vest	accredit	enable

ENCHANT *(verb)*

to put under a magic spell; to fill with intense delight.

Optional Words:

bewitch	captivate	charm	enthrall
fascinate	hypnotize	mesmerize	

ENCIRCLE *(verb)*

to form a circle around; to go around; to surround.

Optional Words:

circle	compass	encompass	involve
gird	hem	ring	halo
wreath			

E

ENCOMPASS *(verb)*

to surround, encircle or contain.

Optional Words:

circle	enclose	envelope	hem
ring	include	embrace	involve
girdle			

ENCOUNTER *(verb)*

to meet, especially by chance or unexpectedly.

Optional Words:

affront	confront	face

ENCOURAGE *(verb)*

to give hope or confidence to; to urge.

Optional Words:

advocate	animate	assist	cheer
favor	foster	further	hearten
influence	inspire	persuade	promote
prompt	spur	sway	motivate

ENDEAR *(verb)*

to cause to be loved.

Optional Words:

attach	charm	delight	win

E

ENDEAVOR *(verb)*

to attempt; to try.

Optional Words:

undertake	seek	strive	push
drive	apply		

ENDORSE *(verb)*

to declare one's approval of.

Optional Words:

authorize	back	notarize	recommend
sanction	sponsor	subscribe	support
underwrite			

ENDOW *(verb)*

to provide with a power, ability or quality.

Optional Words:

accord	bequeath	bestow	confer
equip	grant	provide	supply

ENERGY *(noun)*

the capacity for vigorous activity.

Optional Words:

animation	devotion	exertion	initiative
potency	power	stamina	strength
vigor			

ENGAGE *(verb)*

to promise or pledge.

Optional Words:

book	commission	contract	employ
hire	reserve	retain	schedule

(verb)

to occupy the attention of.

Optional Words:

captivate	engross	immerse

ENGROSS *(verb)*

to occupy the attention of.

Optional Words:

arrest	captivate	enthrall	immerse

ENHANCE *(verb)*

to increase the attractiveness or other qualities of.

Optional Words:

amplify	augment	decorate	embellish
flatter	heighten	intensify	magnify
ornament	reinforce	strengthen	improve

ENJOY *(verb)*

to get pleasure from.

Optional Words:

admire	appreciate	fancy	like
relish	savor		

(verb)

to have as an advantage or benefit.

Optional Words:

own	possess

E

ENLARGE *(verb)*

to make or become larger; to say more about something.

Optional Words:

augment	develop	elaborate	expand
extend	grow	increase	magnify
swell	stretch		

ENLIGHTEN *(verb)*

to give knowledge to.

Optional Words:

edify	educate	explain	tell
direct	instruct	school	teach
train	acquaint	advise	apprise

ENLIVEN *(verb)*

to make more lively.

Optional Words:

animate	brighten	cheer	excite
gladden	stimulate		

ENNOBLE *(verb)*

to make a person or thing noble or dignified.

Optional Words:

exalt	aggrandize	distinguish	glorify
honor	magnify		

ENORMITY *(noun)*

enormous size; magnitude.

Optional Words:

immensity   importance   greatness   tremendousness
vastness   massiveness

ENRAPTURE *(verb)*

to fill with intense delight.

Optional Words:

captivate   charm   delight   enthrall
fascinate   elate   gladden   enchant
please   allure   attract   enravish

ENRICH *(verb)*

to make richer; to improve the quality of.

Optional Words:

adorn   better   decorate   embellish
enhance   fortify   improve

ENTENTE *(noun)*

a friendly understanding between countries.

Optional Words:

cordiality   friendliness   friendship   agreement
alliance   unanimity

E

ENTER *(verb)*

to go or come in or into; to become a member of.

Optional Words:

enroll	infiltrate	ingress	inscribe
invade	join	penetrate	register

ENTERTAIN *(verb)*

to amuse or occupy agreeably.

Optional Words:

cheer	please	treat

(verb)

to consider favorably.

Optional Words:

contemplate	harbor	imagine	receive
welcome			

ENTHRALL *(verb)*

to hold spellbound.

Optional Words:

fascinate	charm	captivate	delight
enchant			

ENTHRONE *(verb)*

to place on a throne, especially with ceremony.

Optional Words:

immortalize	revere	exalt	invest with
deify			

E

ENTHUSIASM *(noun)*

a feeling of eager liking for or interest in something.

Optional Words:

anticipation	ardor	eagerness	excitement
fervor	fire	zeal	passion
élan	devotion		

ENTICE *(verb)*

to attract or persuade by offering something pleasant.

Optional Words:

allure	beguile	fascinate	tempt
invite	captivate		

ENTIRE *(adjective)*

whole; complete.

Optional Words:

absolute	gross	intact	full

ENTITLE *(verb)*

to give a title to.

Optional Words:

call	designate	name

(verb)

to give a right.

Optional Words:

allow	authorize	enable	permit
qualify	designate		

E

....

ENTRANT *(noun)*

one who enters, especially as a competitor.

Optional Words:
joiner   participant

ENTREAT *(verb)*

to request earnestly or emotionally.

Optional Words:
ask   beg   beseech   plead
pray   implore

ENTRUST *(verb)*

to give as a responsibility.

Optional Words:
assign   authorize   delegate
relegate   allot

(verb)
to place a person or thing in a person's care.

Optional Words:
consign   confide

ENUMERATE *(verb)*

to count or name one by one.

Optional Words:
cite   number   specify   tally
itemize   list

E

ENVISAGE *(verb)*

to visualize or imagine.

Optional Words:

conceive   foresee   picture   fancy

EPIGRAM *(noun)*

a short witty saying.

Optional Words:

adage   expression   maxim   motto
proverb   slogan

EQUATE *(verb)*

to consider to be equal or equivalent.

Optional Words:

compare   liken   parallel   equalize
even   assimilate

EQUIP *(verb)*

to supply with what is needed.

Optional Words:

dress   furnish   outfit   provide
gear

E

EQUITY *(noun)*

fairness or impartiality.

Optional Words:
justice   justness

EQUIVALENT *(adjective)*

equal in value, importance or meaning.

Optional Words:
akin	**like**	**similar**	**commensurate**
comparable	**duplicate**		

ESPECIAL *(adjective)*

outstanding; belonging chiefly to one person or thing.

Optional Words:
exceptional	**preeminent**	**supreme**	**surpassing**
dominant	**paramount**	**special**	**preponderant**

ESPOUSE *(verb)*

to give support to (a cause).

Optional Words:
adopt	**advocate**	**champion**	**embrace**
support	**take up**		

ESSENCE *(noun)*

the nature of a thing; an indispensable quality or element.

Optional Words:

principle	substance	virtuality	quintessence
body	marrow	root	soul

ESTABLISH *(verb)*

to show to be true.

Optional Words:

confirm	prove	validate	authenticate
verify			

ESTEEM *(verb)*

to think highly of; to consider or regard.

Optional Words:

cherish	deem	judge	prize
respect	revere	treasure	worship
admire			

ETERNAL *(adjective)*

existing always without beginning or end.

Optional Words:

abiding	ageless	constant	endless
illimitable	immortal	infinite	timeless
perdurable	lasting	perpetual	everlasting
continual			

E

. . . .

EUPHORIA *(noun)*

a feeling of general happiness.

Optional Words:

elation	exaltation	exhilaration	intoxication
ecstasy	glee		

EUREKA *(interjection)*

an exclamation of triumph at a discovery; "I have found it."

EVEN *(adjective)*

equal in degree or amount.

Optional Words:

balanced	constant	uniform	equitable
fair	regular	steady	

EVENT *(noun)*

something that happens, especially something important.

Optional Words:

happening	incident	milestone	circumstance
occurrence	fair	feast	phenomenon
celebration	gala	holiday	fete
festivity			

(noun)

an item in a sports program.

Optional Words:

competition	contest	game	meet

Defined Words and Options
Page 174
. . . .

EVER *(adverb)*

at all times; always; in any possible way.

Optional Words:

always	constantly	continuously	invariably
perpetually	forever		

EVINCE *(verb)*

to indicate; to show that one has a quality.

Optional Words:

disclose	manifest	prove	demonstrate
reveal	exhibit	illustrate	display
signify			

EVOKE *(verb)*

to call up, produce or inspire (memories, feelings or a response).

Optional Words:

draw	extract	invoke	summon
educe	evince	exhort	stimulate
rally	arouse	conjure (up)	awaken

EVOLUTION *(noun)*

the process by which something develops into a different form.

Optional Words:

change	growth	maturation	transformation
progression	flowering	development	

E

· ·

EXACT *(verb)*

to insist on and obtain.

Optional Words:

require   demand   levy

EXCELLENT *(adjective)*

having good qualities in a high degree; extremely good.

Optional Words:

admirable	estimable	exquisite	distinguished
fine	sublime	superb	superior
wonderful	capital	choice	blue-ribbon
first-rate	first-class	five-star	prime
premium			

EXCEPTIONAL *(adjective)*

forming an exception; very unusual or outstandingly good.

Optional Words:

novel	rare	superior	phenomenal
unique	prime	premium	remarkable
singular	distinct	notable	extraordinary

EXCESS *(noun)*

the exceeding of due limits.

Optional Words:

lavishness   luxury   overabundance   surplus

E

EXCITE *(verb)*

to rouse the feelings of; to cause a person to feel strongly or eagerly.

Optional Words:

delight	electrify	exhilarate	inflame
inspire	stir	thrill	galvanize
move	pique	prime	stimulate
innovate			

EXCITEMENT *(noun)*

the act of exciting; the arousal of feelings.

Optional Words:

action	hubbub	stir	enthusiasm
movement	exhilaration	emotion	stimulation
drama	melodrama	provocation	commotion
flurry	bustle	to-do	animation
passion	flutter	intensity	vivacity

EXCLAIM *(verb)*

to cry out or utter suddenly from pleasure or surprise.

Optional Words:

cry	shout	vociferate	yell
interject			

EXCLUSIVE *(adjective)*

a special grouping, carefully selected.

Optional Words:

elite	select	chosen	stylish
chic			

E

EXCUSE *(verb)*

to pardon.

Optional Words:

exempt	forgive	free	relieve
remit			

EXECUTE *(verb)*

to carry out or produce; to put a plan into effect.

Optional Words:

administer	do	enact	perform
render			

EXECUTIVE *(noun)*

a person or group that has administrative or managerial powers or that has authority to put the laws or agreements of a government into effect.

Optional Words:

director	manager	official	supervisor
boss	officer		

EXEMPLARY *(adjective)*

serving as an example.

Optional Words:

illustrative	model	symbolic	representative
typical	ideal	pure	righteous
virtuous	admirable	prototypic	paradigmatic

E

EXERT *(verb)*

to bring a quality or influence into use.

Optional Words:
apply   **employ**   **exercise**   **expend**
wield

EXHIBIT *(verb)*

to display; to present for the public to see.

Optional Words:
demonstrate   **expose**   **feature**   **parade**
present

EXHILARATE *(verb)*

to make very happy or lively.

Optional Words:
cheer   **delight**   **elate**   **enliven**
gladden   **invigorate**   **rejuvenate**   **stimulate**

EXPAND *(verb)*

to increase in bulk or importance.

Optional Words:
augment   **develop**   **elaborate**   **enlarge**
explain   **extend**

E

EXPECT *(verb)*

to wish for and be confident that one will receive.

Optional Words:

anticipate	assume	envision	foresee
imagine	presume	suppose	

EXPEDIENT *(adjective)*

suitable for a particular purpose.

Optional Words:

beneficial	convenient	fitting	appropriate
helpful	proper	suitable	advantageous
useful	practical		

(noun)

a means of achieving something.

EXPEDITE *(verb)*

to hurry the progress of; to perform quickly.

Optional Words:

accelerate	advance	facilitate	further
hasten	hurry	promote	quicken

EXPERIENCE *(noun)*

actual observation of facts or events; activity or practice in doing something; skill or knowledge gained from doing something.

Optional Words:

background	education	practice	seasoning
training	familiarity		

E

EXPERT *(noun)*

a person with great knowledge or skill in a particular area.

Optional Words:

ace   artist   authority   professional
master   specialist

EXPLAIN *(verb)*

to make plain or clear; to show the meaning of.

Optional Words:

decipher   define   illustrate   demonstrate
illuminate   interpret   reveal

EXPLODE *(verb)*

to expand suddenly because of the release of internal energy.

Optional Words:

burst   blowup   mushroom   energize

EXPLORE *(verb)*

to examine or investigate.

Optional Words:

inquire   prospect   scout   search
survey   venture

E

. . . .

EXPONENT *(noun)*

a person who sets out the facts or interprets something.

Optional Words:

advocate	champion	expounder	proponent
promoter	upholder	partisan	supporter

EXPOSE *(verb)*

to make visible; to reveal.

Optional Words:

bare	display	exhibit

EXPOSÉ *(noun)*

an orderly statement of facts.

Optional Words:

revelation	broadcast	advertisement

EXPOUND *(verb)*

to set forth or explain in detail.

Optional Words:

define	state	interpret	exemplify
construe	explicate	present	clarify
delineate	illustrate	describe	

E

EXPRESS *(adjective)*

definitely stated, not merely implied; going or sent quickly; designed for high speed.

Optional Words:
precise   fast

(verb)
to make known; to put into words.

Optional Words:

declare	depict	represent	communicate
signify	symbolize	utter	verbalize
voice	interpret	state	

EXQUISITE *(adjective)*

having special beauty or excellent discrimination.

Optional Words:

beautiful	chic	dainty	elegant
striking	fine	flawless	immaculate
lovely	precise	impeccable	

EXTEND *(verb)*

to make longer in space or time; to stretch out; to offer or grant.

Optional Words:

advance	augment	broaden	continue
elongate	enlarge	increase	lengthen
overhang	project	prolong	protrude
range	reach	expand	

E

EXTOL *(verb)*

to praise enthusiastically.

Optional Words:

celebrate   **glorify**   **hail**   **laud**
exalt

EXTRA *(adjective)*

more than is usual or expected.

Optional Words:

accessory   **additional**   **auxiliary**   **supernumerary**
excess   **further**   **superfluous**   **supplementary**
surplus

EXTRAVAGANZA *(noun)*

a lavish, spectacular production.

Optional Words:

exposition   **pageant**   **special event**

EXTREME *(adjective)*

very great or intense.

Optional Words:

outlandish   **outrageous**   **utmost**   **peak**
top

EXTROVERT *(noun)*

a person more interested in the people and things around him than in his own thoughts and feelings; a lively sociable person.

Optional Words:
mingler   **mixer**   **socializer**   **life-of-the-party**

EXUBERANT *(adjective)*

full of high spirits, very lively.

Optional Words:
animated   **zesty**   **effervescent**   **enthusiastic** **exhilarated**

EXULT *(verb)*

to rejoice greatly; to take great delight.

Optional Words:
glorify   **rejoice**   **revel**   **jubilate** **triumph**   **celebrate**

EYE-OPENER *(noun)*

a fact or circumstance that brings enlightenment or great surprise.

F

F

Section Index

F

F

FABRICATE *(verb)*

to construct; to manufacture.

Optional Words:

assemble	build	concoct	erect
formulate	invent	fashion	form
produce	shape	create	devise

FABULOUS *(adjective)*

incredibly great, wonderful or marvelous.

Optional Words:

amazing	astonishing	celebrated	fantastic
legendary	superb	astounding	extravagant
inordinate	outrageous	stupendous	prodigious

FACET *(noun)*

each aspect of a situation.

Optional Words:

part	point	side	phase
angle			

FACILITATE *(verb)*

to make easy.

Optional Words:

advance	aid	assist	ease
encourage	expedite	promote	simplify

F

FACT *(noun)*

something known to have happened, to be true or to exist.

Optional Words:
actuality   **certainty**   **reality**   **truth**

FAIR *(adjective)*

just; in accordance with the rules.

Optional Words:
equitable   **honest**   **impartial**   **upright**
lawful   **objective**   **reasonable**

FAITH *(noun)*

reliance or trust in a person or thing.

Optional Words:
confidence   **expectation** **hope**   **credence**
credit   **dependence**

(noun)
belief without evidence.

Optional Words:
conviction

F

FAMILIAR *(adjective)*

having close knowledge; well-acquainted;well-known.

Optional Words:
famous

(adjective)
often seen or experienced.

Optional Words:

accepted	accustomed	acquainted	commonplace
everyday	frequent	habitual	intimate
ordinary			

FAMILY *(noun)*

all the descendants of a common ancestor.

Optional Words:

ancestry	blood	brood	forefathers
kin	offspring	progeny	relations
relatives	clan	folk	house
lineage	tribe	dynasty	

FAMOUS *(adjective)*

known to many people.

Optional Words:

acclaimed	celebrated	eminent	distinguished
famed	illustrious	noted	prominent
renowned	well-known	popular	notable

FAN *(noun)*

an enthusiastic admirer or supporter; a lover of something.

Optional Words:

booster	devotee	enthusiast	follower
zealot	buff		

F

....

FANCY *(noun)*

the power of imagining things, especially of a fantastic sort; a liking.

Optional Words:

affection	caprice	fantasy	illusion
inclination	notion	illusion	whim
pleasure	velleity		

(adjective)

ornamental or elaborate.

Optional Words:

decorative	elegant	ornate	trimmed
embellished	bedecked	charming	luxurious
scrumptious	stylish	baroque	gilded
beautiful	garnished	enhanced	adorned
frilly	rich	extravagant	flamboyant
opulent			

FANFARE *(noun)*

a short, showy or ceremonious sounding (of trumpets).

Optional Words:

display	array	panoply	pomp

FANTASTIC *(adjective)*

absurdly fanciful; remarkable or excellent.

Optional Words:

chimerical	extravagant	extreme	extraordinary
great	incredible	marvelous	phenomenal
tremendous	ingenious	clever	heroic
magnificent	superb	famous	majestic
monumental	outstanding	fabulous	awesome
exquisite	amazing		

FANTASY *(noun)*

imagination, especially when producing fanciful ideas.

Optional Words:

apparition	dream	fabrication	fancy
fiction	illusion	invention	mirage
phantom	vision	reverie	whim
aspiration	hope	phantasm	chimera

FASCINATE *(verb)*

to attract and hold the interest of; to charm greatly.

Optional Words:

appeal to	captivate	engross	enthrall
interest	intrigue	mesmerize	spellbind
attract	allure	draw	excite

FASHION *(noun)*

a manner or way of doing something.

Optional Words:

convention	custom	fad	method
mode	style	tradition	trend
vogue			

FAST *(adjective)*

moving or done quickly.

Optional Words:

fleet	quick	rapid	alert
brisk	keen	lively	snappy
hasty	nimble	agile	expiditious

F

· ·

FASTIDIOUS *(adjective)*

having or showing attention to detail; choosing only what is good.

Optional Words:

exacting	meticulous	particular

FATE *(noun)*

a power thought to control all events.

Optional Words:

destiny	fortune	future	predetermination
lot	luck	kismet	predestination

FAVOR *(noun)*

liking, goodwill or approval; an act that is kindly or helpful, beyond what is due or usual.

Optional Words:

gift	benefaction	sacrifice	partiality
leaning			

(verb)

to regard or treat with favor.

Optional Words:

accept	approbation	aid	assistance
backing	cooperation		

FEASIBLE *(adjective)*

able to be done; possible.

Optional Words:

achievable	attainable	obtainable	practical
viable	workable	doable	suitable
likely	plausible		

· · · · · · · · · · · · · · · · · ·

F

FEAT *(noun)*

a remarkable action or achievement.

Optional Words:

act	deed	enterprise	accomplishment
performance	conquest	triumph	consummation

FEEL *(verb)*

to be conscious of; to be aware of.

Optional Words:

believe	empathize	perceive	experience
presume	sense	think	comprehend

FEELING *(noun)*

the sense of touch.

Optional Words:

sensation	reaction	response

(noun)

general state of mind or emotion.

Optional Words:

empathy	clemency	sensitivity	commiseration
reaction	affection	sympathy	synesthesia
intuition	awareness	response	appreciation
passion	conviction	sentiment	compassion
affinity	accord	rapport	understanding
warmth	emotion		

FELICITATE *(verb)*

to wish joy or happiness to; to make happy.

Optional Words:

recommend	congratulate	compliment	salute

F

FELICITOUS *(adjective)*

well-chosen or apt.

Optional Words:

applicable	appropriate	germane	pertinent
well-timed	opportune	relevant	convincing
fitting	just		

FELICITY *(noun)*

the state of being happy; great happiness; a pleasing manner or style.

Optional Words:

bliss	delight	gratification	joy
pleasure	rapture	satisfaction	

FELLOWSHIP *(noun)*

friendly association with others; companionship.

Optional Words:

brotherhood	comradeship	fraternity	friendship
league	order	society	association
club	solidarity		

FEND *(verb)*

to provide a livelihood for; to look after.

Optional Words:

support	protect	secure	shield

FESTIVAL *(noun)*

a day or time of religious or other celebration; a periodically given series of performances of music, drama or films.

Optional Words:

carnival	fair	feast	gala
holiday	jamboree	jubilee	event
fete	fiesta	party	festivity

FETCH *(verb)*

to go for and bring back.

Optional Words:

get	bring	regain	retrieve

FETE *(noun)*

a festival; an outdoor entertainment or sale, usually to raise funds for a cause or charity.

Optional Words:

banquet	celebration	feast	festival
party	event		

FIESTA *(noun)*

a holiday or religious festival, especially in Spanish-speaking countries.

Optional Words:

carnival	party	event	celebration
gala	jamboree	holiday	feast

F

FILL (verb)

to make or become full.

Optional Words:

blow up	expand	furnish	fuel
fulfill	gorge	inflate	load
pack	provide	saturate	supply

(noun)

enough to satisfy a person's appetite or desire.

Optional Words:

enough	share

FIND (verb)

to discover by search.

Optional Words:

detect	locate	distinguish	identify
encounter	spot	sight	note

(verb)

to succeed in obtaining.

Optional Words:

achieve	acquire	attain

FINE (adjective)

of high quality or great merit.

Optional Words:

choice	elegant	exquisite	precise
refined	splendid	superb	superior
excellent			

FINESSE *(noun)*

delicate manipulation; tact and cleverness in dealing with a situation.

Optional Words:

delicacy	**diplomacy**	**refinement**	**savoir-faire**
tact	**taste**		

FINISH *(verb)*

to bring or come to an end; to complete a task or race.

Optional Words:

achieve	**accomplish**	**conclude**	**consummate**
fulfill			

FIRM *(adjective)*

hard or solid.

Optional Words:

steady	**stiff**	**strong**	**rigid**
stable			

(adjective)

securely fixed or established.

Optional Words:

anchored	**definite**	**determined**	**moored**
resolute	**stable**	**staunch**	**steadfast**
steady	**strong**		

FIRST *(adjective)*

coming before all others.

Optional Words:

basic	**earliest**	**initial**	**fundamental**
leading	**main**	**original**	**paramount**
preeminent	**primary**	**principal**	**foremost**
inaugural	**pioneer**	**founding**	

F

FIRST-CLASS *(adjective)*

of the best quality.

Optional Words:

excellent	capital	fine	first-rate
five-star	superior	top	topnotch

FIT *(adjective)*

suitable or well-adapted for something.

Optional Words:

appropriate	capable	competent	proper
qualified	suitable		

FLASH *(verb)*

to give out a brief or intermittent bright light.

Optional Words:

blaze	blink	flicker	glitter
sparkle	twinkle		

FLEXIBLE *(adjective)*

able to be changed to suit circumstances.

Optional Words:

affable	agile	amiable	changeable
compliant	elastic	lithe	pliant
supple	resilient	springy	amenable
docile	adaptable	yielding	moldable

F

FLOURISH *(verb)*

to thrive in growth or development; to be successful.

Optional Words:

flower	grow	increase	prosper
succeed	wax	aggrandize	better
swell	augment	improve	build
gain	amplify	advance	multiply

FLOW *(verb)*

to proceed steadily, continuously, smoothly and evenly.

Optional Words:

circulate	course	eddy	pour
roll			

FLUENT *(adjective)*

able to speak smoothly and readily.

Optional Words:

articulate	eloquent	loquacious	well-versed

FLUKE *(noun)*

a stroke of good luck.

Optional Words:

chance	miracle	fortuitous

F

··

FOCUS *(verb)*

to concentrate; to direct attention.

Optional Words:

aim	center	converge	fix
direct	rivet		

FOLD *(noun)*

an established body of people with the same beliefs or aims; the members of a church.

Optional Words:

flock	family	group	congregation

FOLLOW *(verb)*

to go or come after.

Optional Words:

ensue	pursue	trace	trail
supervene			

(verb)

to grasp the meaning of or understand; to take an interest in the progress of.

Optional Words:

regard	comprehend

(verb)

to happen as a result; to be necessarily true in consequence of something else.

Optional Words:

succeed

FOND *(adjective)*

affectionate, loving or doting.

Optional Words:

cherished	tender	dear	devoted

●●●●●●●●●●●●●●●●●

FONDLE *(verb)*

to touch or stroke lovingly.

Optional Words:

caress	cuddle	embrace	hug
nuzzle	pet	snuggle	nestle

FORBEARANCE *(noun)*

the act of being tolerant.

Optional Words:

mercy	restraint	self-control	temperance
longanimity	endurance	leniency	charity
grace	clemency	patience	

FORCE *(noun)*

strength and power; intense effort or effectiveness.

Optional Words:

energy	impact	import	pressure
value	vigor	vitality	significance
weight			

FORE *(adjective)*

situated in front.

Optional Words:

beginning	first	initial	head

F

FORECAST *(verb)*

to tell in advance.

Optional Words:

anticipate	calculate	determine	divine
expect	foresee	gauge	predict
project	prophesy		

FOREMOST *(adjective)*

most advanced in position or rank; most important.

Optional Words:

chief	paramount	preeminent	principal
supreme	first	dominant	primary
earliest	initial	leading	main

FORESEE *(verb)*

to be aware of or realize beforehand.

Optional Words:

anticipate	await	expect	envision
foretell	predict	prophesy	visualize

FORTE *(noun)*

a person's strong point.

Optional Words:

aptitude	proficiency	specialty	strength
talent	skill	gift	

F

FORTH *(adverb)*

out into view; onward or forward.

Optional Words:

ahead	farther	outward	visibly

FORTIFY *(verb)*

to strengthen mentally or morally; to increase the vigor of.

Optional Words:

augment	brace	encourage	enhance
enrich	hearten	reassure	reinforce
sustain	energize	ready	invigorate
rally	rouse	stir	supplement
prepare	steel		

FORTUNE *(noun)*

the events that chance brings to a person or undertaking.

Optional Words:

destiny	fate	luck	godsend
kismet	fortuity	lottery	providence
fluke			

(noun)

prosperity or success; a great amount of wealth.

Optional Words:

wealth	riches	opulence	assets
bounty	prosperity	treasure	affluence
bonanza			

F

FORWARD *(adjective)*

at or near the front.

Optional Words:
onward   fore

(verb)

to send or promote; to help onward.

Optional Words:

advance	**progress**	**encourage**	**foster**
further	**promote**	**champion**	**support**

FOUNDATION *(noun)*

the underlying basis or idea on which something is based.

Optional Words:

base	**groundwork**	**essence**	**infrastructure**
origination	**source**		

FREE *(adjective)*

self-determining controls of physical, moral and legal influence.

Optional Words:

available	**liberated**	**separate**	**emancipated**
clear	**loose**	**independent**	

FREQUENT *(adjective)*

happening or appearing often.

Optional Words:

constant	**continual**	**customary**	**habitual**
numerous	**recurrent**	**regular**	**usual**

FRESH *(adjective)*

newly made, produced or gathered; newly arrived; new or different.

Optional Words:

creative	novel	original	contemporary
recent	unique	modern	neoteric
vivid	natural	raw	

FRIEND *(noun)*

a person with whom one feels mutual affection; a helper.

Optional Words:

ally	benefactor	buddy	companion
compatriot	comrade	confederate	confidant
pal	patron	amigo	intimate
sidekick	accomplice	mate	cohort
chum	crony		

FRISK *(verb)*

to leap or skip playfully.

Optional Words:

dance	frolic	play	caper
cavort	rollick	romp	gambol

FRUITFUL *(adjective)*

producing good results.

Optional Words:

blooming	efficacious	fertile	flourishing
productive	profitable	prolific	successful
thriving	well-spent	worthwhile	proliferate

F

FRUITION (noun)

the fulfillment of hopes; results attained by work.

Optional Words:

achievement	attainment	completion	contentment
gratification	realization	satisfaction	accomplishment

FULFILL (verb)

to carry out a task; to make come true.

Optional Words:

effect	satisfy	meet	accomplish
achieve			

FULL (adjective)

holding or having as much as the limits will allow; having much or many.

Optional Words:

abounding	abundant	brimming	bursting
complete	crowded	entire	packed
replete	saturated	swarming	teeming
whole	awash	stuffed	

FUN (noun)

light-hearted amusement.

Optional Words:

frolic	gaiety	game	jest
joke	merriment	play	pleasure
sport	joviality	recreation	entertainment

FUNCTION *(noun)*

the special activity or purpose of a person or thing.

Optional Words:

role   **use**   **objective**

(noun)

an important social or official ceremony.

Optional Words:

fete   **occasion**   **party**   **reception**
event

FUTURE *(adjective)*

the time yet to come; prospect or outlook.

Optional Words:

coming   **imminent**   **impending**   **projected**
hereafter

G

G

Section Index

G

GAIETY *(noun)*

cheerfulness; a happy and lighthearted manner.

Optional Words:

animation	cheer	festivity	jollity
joviality	merriment	mirth	revelry
vivacity	happiness	exhilaration	

GAIN *(verb)*

to obtain, especially something desirable; to make a profit.

Optional Words:

achieve	acquire	attain	augment
grow	realize	succeed	annex
land	procure	secure	

GALA *(noun)*

a festive occasion or a special event.

Optional Words:

carnival	celebration	festival	holiday
jubilee	party	event	ball
fete			

GALLANT *(adjective)*

possessing an intrepid spirit.

Optional Words:

stately	imposing	courteous	dashing
courtly	gracious	heroic	urbane
suave	attentive	brave	considerate
bold			

G

·····························

GALORE *(adjective)*

in plenty.

Optional Words:

abundant	profuse	multiple	plentiful
ample	bounteous	liberal	lavish

GAME *(noun)*

a form of play or sport.

Optional Words:

amusement	competition	contest	diversion
match	meet	pastime	entertainment
recreation	tournament	event	

GARNISH *(verb)*

to decorate (especially food for the table).

Optional Words:

array	beautify	bedeck	embroider
embellish	ornament	dress (up)	trim

GATHER *(verb)*

to bring or come together; to collect; to obtain gradually.

Optional Words:

accumulate	assemble	meet	throng
unite	cluster	amass	

GAY *(adjective)*

lighthearted and full of fun; bright-colored; dressed or decorated in bright colors.

Optional Words:

airy	blithe	lively	merry
sunny	vivacious	festive	gleeful
jolly	jovial	spirited	cheerful
happy			

GEE *(interjection)*

a mild exclamation.

Optional Words:

wow	yea	golly	gosh

GENERATE *(verb)*

to bring into existence; to produce.

Optional Words:

beget	create	engender	father
form	induce	initiate	make
procreate	propagate	bear	hatch

GENEROUS *(adjective)*

giving or ready to give freely.

Optional Words:

beneficent	charitable	liberal	greathearted
altruistic	munificent	giving	humanitarian
benevolent	helpful	openhanded	magnanimous
copious	philanthropic		

G

GENIAL *(adjective)*

kindly, pleasant and cheerful.

Optional Words:

agreeable	affable	amiable	cheery
convivial	cordial	courteous	jovial
mild	gracious	sweet	

GENTEEL *(adjective)*

well-bred or refined; elegant and polite.

Optional Words:

stylish	fashionable	cultivated	distinguished
polished	urbane	graceful	chivalrous
gentlemanly	knightly	ladylike	noble
mannerly	courteous	cultured	civil

GENTLE *(adjective)*

mild in disposition; refined in manners.

Optional Words:

tame	docile	soft	moderate
polite	affable		

GIANT *(adjective)*

of a kind that is very large in size.

Optional Words:

colossal	enormous	gigantic	immense
mammoth	massive	mighty	titanic
elephantine	gargantuan	monstrous	prodigious
hulking	huge	stupendous	

GIFT *(noun)*

a thing given or received without payment.

Optional Words:

benefaction	contribution	donation	endowment
gratuity	offering	present	

(noun)

a natural ability.

Optional Words:

aptitude	flair	genius	talent
instinct	forte	propensity	specialty

GIVE *(verb)*

present, administer or supply.

Optional Words:

allot	assign	award	confer
contribute	deliver	dispense	distribute
donate	endow	furnish	grant
provide	offer	disburse	

GLAD *(adjective)*

pleased; expressing or giving joy.

Optional Words:

animated	cheerful	delighted	eager
elated	exhilarated	happy	joyful
gratified			

GLAMOUR *(noun)*

alluring beauty; attractive and exciting qualities.

Optional Words:

allure	appeal	aura	elegance
flair	style	magnetism	

G

GLARING *(adjective)*

bright and dazzling.

Optional Words:

blinding	brilliant	harsh	intense
radiant	sparkling	flashing	shining

GLEAM *(noun)*

a brief show of glimmering light.

Optional Words:

brilliance	iridescence	luster	sheen
shine	beam	radiance	

GLEE *(noun)*

lively or triumphant joy.

Optional Words:

delight	jollity	joy	merriment
mirth	happiness	gaiety	

GLIDE *(verb)*

to move along smoothly.

Optional Words:

coast	drift	float	fly
sail	slide	soar	

GLITTER *(verb)*

to sparkle.

Optional Words:

scintillate	shimmer	shine	illuminate
flash	glow	gleam	radiate

GLORY *(noun)*

fame and honor won by great deeds; adoration and praise in worship; beauty and magnificence; a thing deserving praise and honor.

Optional Words:

brilliance	distinction	eminence	fame
grandeur	homage	illumination	luster
majesty	radiance		

GLOSS *(noun)*

the shine on a smooth surface.

Optional Words:

glow	luster	sheen	shine
radiance	sparkle		

GLOW *(verb)*

to have a warm or flushed look, color or feeling; very enthusiastic or favorable.

Optional Words:

beam	bloom	blush	flush
gleam	shine		

(noun)

a glowing state, look or feeling.

Optional Words:

beam	bloom	blush	flush
radiance	gleam	shine	incandescence

G

GO *(verb)*

to begin to move.

Optional Words:

advance	depart	leave	perform
proceed	progress	run	travel
walk			

GOD *(proper noun)*

the one Supreme Being, self-existent and eternal; the infinite creator, sustainer and ruler of the universe; (conceived of as omniscient, good and almighty).

Optional Words:
Lord

GODSEND *(noun)*

a piece of unexpected good fortune.

Optional Words:

blessing	boon	gift	stroke of luck

GOLD *(noun)*

something very good or precious.

Optional Words:

treasure	brilliance	valuable

G

GOLLY *(interjection)*

an exclamation of surprise.

Optional Words:

gee	wow	yea	gosh

GOOD *(adjective)*

having the right or desirable properties; morally correct and virtuous; well-behaved; enjoyable or beneficial.

Optional Words:

just	competent	considerate	conscientious
kindly	dependable	generous	favorable
honest	noble	obedient	respectable
pure	qualified	reliable	satisfactory
suitable	right	proper	

(adverb)
well entirely.

(noun)
that which is morally right; a profit or benefit.

GORGEOUS *(adjective)*

richly colored or magnificent; very pleasant or beautiful.

Optional Words:

dazzling	ravishing	splendid	resplendent
stunning	desirable	grand	elegant
becoming	winning	alluring	appealing
attractive	glorious		

GOSH *(injection)*

an exclamation of surprise.

Optional Words:

golly	gee	wow	yea

G

· ·

GOSPEL *(noun)*

a narrative of Christ's teachings and life as given in the first books of the New Testament.

(noun)
a thing one may safely believe or a set of principles that one believes in; good news or tidings, especially the message of salvation preached by Jesus Christ and the apostles.

Optional Words:

certainty	credo	creed	doctrine
fact	teachings	truth	verity

GOVERN *(verb)*

to rule with authority; to conduct the affairs of a country or an organization; to keep under control, influence or direct.

Optional Words:

administer	control	manage	oversee
regulate	reign	supervise	guide

GRAB *(verb)*

to grasp suddenly.

Optional Words:

grip	catch	clutch	nab
snatch			

(noun)
a sudden clutch or an attempt to seize.

Optional Words:

grip	catch	clutch

G

GRACE *(noun)*

the quality of being attractive, especially in movement, manner or design.

Optional Words:

agility	dexterity	ease	goodness
nimbleness	poise	polish	refinement
style	suppleness	virtue	elegance

(noun)

favor or goodwill.

Optional Words:

blessing	charity	compassion

GRAND *(adjective)*

splendid and magnificent; the highest rank; dignified and imposing.

Optional Words:

grandiose	great	immense	majestic
noble	regal	stately	

GRANT *(verb)*

to give or allow as a privilege; to give formally or transfer legally; to admit or agree that something is true.

Optional Words:

accord	award	bestow	concede
give	profess	suppose	

G

GRASP *(verb)*

to seize and hold firmly, especially with one's hands or arms.

Optional Words:

catch	clasp	clench	clutch
nab			

(verb)
to comprehend.

Optional Words:

perceive   understand

GRATEFUL *(adjective)*

feeling or showing that one values a kindness or benefit received.

Optional Words:

appreciative	indebted	obliged	pleased
thankful	beholden	gratified	

GRATIFY *(verb)*

to give pleasure to; to satisfy wishes.

Optional Words:

appease	indulge	mollify	soothe
humor	delight		

GRATIS *(adverb & adjective)*

free of charge; given or done without payment.

Optional Words:

donated	free	voluntary	complimentary
willingly			

GRATITUDE *(noun)*

being grateful.

Optional Words:

thanks   appreciation thankfulness acknowledgment
indebtedness

GRAVITATE *(verb)*

to move or be attracted toward, as though drawn by a powerful source.

Optional Words:

incline

GREAT *(adjective)*

much above average size, amount or intensity; of remarkable ability or character; important; very enjoyable or satisfactory.

Optional Words:

eminent	excellent	weighty	distinguished
vast	famous	heroic	magnificent
huge	immense	majestic	monumental
noble	outstanding	prominent	exceptional
royal	spacious	superb	transcendent

GREETING *(noun)*

words or gestures used to greet a person.

Optional Words:

best wishes	reception	regards	compliments
respects	salutation	welcome	

G

●●●●●●●●●●●●●●●●●●●●●●●●●●●

GREGARIOUS *(adjective)*
fond of company.
Optional Words:
**convivial   friendly   outgoing   companionable
sociable**

GRIN *(verb)*
to smile broadly, showing the teeth.
Optional Words:
beam   smile   radiate

(noun)
a broad smile.
Optional Words:
smile

GRIP *(verb)*
to take a firm hold of.
Optional Words:
clasp   clench   clutch   grasp

(noun)
a firm grasp or hold.
Optional Words:
clasp   clench   clutch   grasp

G

GROW *(verb)*

to increase in size; to progress by maturity; to flourish and thrive.

Optional Words:

flower	prosper	succeed	change
cultivate	produce	propagate	raise
develop	expand	become	burgeon
heighten	augment	amplify	bloom
improve	evolve	better	enhance
inflate	enlarge	swell	build
snowball	enrich		

GUARANTEE *(verb)*

a formal promise to do what has been agreed.

Optional Words:

pledge	warranty	word	oath
surety	assurance	covenant	testimony
pact	bond	vow	assertion
contract	promise		

(verb)

to promise or state with certainty.

Optional Words:

pledge	promise	vow

GUARD *(verb)*

to watch over and protect; to keep safe or in check.

Optional Words:

cover	defend	escort	patrol
shelter	shield	bulwark	fortify
buffer	bumper	champion	preserve
protect			

H

Section Index

H

. . . .

HA-HA *(interjection)*

an outburst of laughter; surprise or joy.

Optional Words:
wow   **gee**   **ho-ho**

HAIL *(interjection)*

an exclamation of greeting.

(verb)
to greet; to call to order; to attract attention; to signal to and summon.

Optional Words:
greet   **signal**   **welcome**

(verb)
to commend.

Optional Words:

acclaim	**applaud**	**cheer**	**honor**
praise	**salute**	**compliment**	**recommend**

HALLMARK *(noun)*

a distinguishing characteristic; any mark proving genuineness or excellence.

Optional Words:

symbol	**sign**	**certification**	**endorsement**
signet	**stamp of approval**		**seal of approval**

. . . .

H

HALLOW *(verb)*

to make holy; to honor as holy.

Optional Words:

consecrate	dedicate	enshrine	honor
revere	sanctify	venerate	worship
praise	salute	glorify	exalt
extol	eulogize	bless	laud
celebrate			

HALO *(noun)*

a disc or ring of light shown round the head of a sacred figure in paintings, etc.; a disc of diffused light around a luminous body such as the sun or moon.

Optional Words:

nimbus	aura	corona	aureola
radiance			

HAND *(noun)*

active help; a pledge, especially of marriage; a round of applause.

Optional Words:

approval	assistance	engagement	encouragement
aid			

HANDSOME *(adjective)*

agreeable to the eye or to good taste; of liberal dimensions or proportions; marked by magnanimity or generosity.

Optional Words:

attractive	beautiful	comely	good-looking
fair	pretty	bounteous	bountiful
generous	munificent	openhanded	large
majestic	freehanded		

H

HANKER *(verb)*

to crave; to feel a longing.

Optional Words:
desire   wish   long

HAP *(noun)*

a casual occurrence.

Optional Words:
chance   luck   happening   good fortune

HAPPEN *(verb)*

to occur; to have the good fortune to do something.

Optional Words:
befall   ensue   transpire   come to pass
take place

HAPPY *(adjective)*

feeling or showing pleasure or contentment.

Optional Words:
cheerful   delighted   glad   light-hearted
content   joyful

(adjective)
fortunate.

Optional Words:
fortuitous   lucky   opportune

H

....

HARDIHOOD *(noun)*

boldness or daring.

Optional Words:

intrepidity   grit   moxie   courage

HARMONIOUS *(adjective)*

forming a pleasing or consistent whole.

Optional Words:

agreeable   compatible   accord   concord
mellifluous   symmetric   unified   peaceful
balanced   accordant   fluent   harmonic
complimentary

(adjective)

sweet sounding or tuneful.

Optional Words:

euphonious   melodious   harmonic   synchronized

HASTE *(noun)*

quickness of movement or action.

Optional Words:

speed   swiftness   dispatch   acceleration
rapidity   hurry

HAVEN *(noun)*

a refuge.

Optional Words:

retreat   sanctuary   shelter   home
port

• • • • • • • • • • • • • • • •

H

HEAD *(noun)*

the chief person of a group or organization.

Optional Words:
commander   director   leader   manager

(verb)

to be at the head or top of; to move in a certain direction.

Optional Words:
supervise   direct

HEALTHY *(adjective)*

beneficial; functioning well.

Optional Words:
fit   hale   hearty   robust
sound   vigorous   well

HEAP *(verb)*

to load with large quantities.

Optional Words:
accumulate   amass   cluster   congregate
group

HEARKEN *(verb)*

to listen, hear or heed.

Optional Words:
attend

H

HEART *(noun)*

the center of a person's emotions, affections or thoughts.
Optional Words:
soul   spirit

(noun)
the ability to feel emotion.
Optional Words:
compassion concern   sympathy

(noun)
courage or enthusiasm.
Optional Words:
valor   nerve   bravery

(noun)
the innermost part of a thing.
Optional Words:
core   essence

HEARTEN *(verb)*

to make a person feel encouraged.
Optional Words:

animate	enhearten	embolden	cheer
inspirit	support	strengthen	assure
boost	reinforce		

HEARTFELT *(adjective)*

felt deeply or earnestly.
Optional Words:

earnest	fervent	genuine	wholehearted
profound	sincere		

HEARTY *(adjective)*

showing warmth of feeling; enthusiastic and vigorous; strong or large.

Optional Words:

cordial	fervent	friendly	healthy
robust	sincere	sound	wholehearted

HEAVE *(verb)*

to throw.

Optional Words:

cast	hurl	pitch	toss
launch	sling	fire	fling

HEAVEN *(noun)*

the abode of God; the dwelling place or state of existence of righteous souls after their life on earth; a place or state of supreme bliss; something delightful, divine and pleasing.

Optional Words:

nirvana	paradise	rapture	enchantment
Zion	eternity	glory	promised land
utopia	here after		

HEAVYWEIGHT *(noun)*

a person of great influence.

Optional Words:

notable	leader	VIP

H

HEED *(verb)*

to pay attention to.

Optional Words:

consider	listen	respect	bear in mind
notice	thought	follow	care

(noun)

careful attention.

Optional Words:

thought	care

HEFTY *(adjective)*

big and strong; large and heavy; powerful.

Optional Words:

beefy	burly	husky	muscular
robust	stout		

HEGEMONY *(noun)*

leadership, especially by one country.

Optional Words:

ascendancy	dominance	preeminence	superiority

HEIGH-HO *(interjection)*

an exclamation of surprise or curiosity.

HEIGHTEN *(verb)*

to make or become higher or more intense.

Optional Words:

elevate	enhance	increase	augment
aggrandize	boost	compound	enlarge
magnify	extend	multiply	raise
lift			

HELP *(verb)*

to make it easier for a person to do something or for a thing to happen; to be useful; to do something for the benefit of someone in need.

Optional Words:

abet	aid	assist	better
ease	expedite	extricate	facilitate
improve	serve	support	

HERALD *(noun)*

an official in former times who made announcements and carried messages from a ruler; a person or thing indicating the approach of something.

Optional Words:

courier	crier	envoy	forerunner
messenger	runner	harbinger	announcement
presage	precursor		

HERO *(noun)*

someone who is admired for brave or noble deeds; the chief male character in a story, play or poem.

Optional Words:

champion	idol	superstar	chief
leader	mentor		

H

HEY *(interjection)*

an exclamation calling attention or expressing surprise.

Optional Words:

yea   wow   hello

HEYDAY *(noun)*

the time of greatest success, prosperity, vibrancy and vigor.

Optional Words:

bloom   prime   prime of life

HIGH *(adjective)*

extending far upwards; extending above the normal or
average level; ranking above others in importance or
quality; very favorable, noble or virtuous.

Optional Words:

elevated	eminent	great	distinguished
extravagant	lofty	prominent	significant
tall	towering	powerful	soaring
intense	extreme	gigantic	colossal

HIGHBROW *(adjective)*

very intellectual; cultured.

Optional Words:

bookish   scholarly   cerebral

HIGHLIGHT *(noun)*

the brightest or most outstanding feature of something.

Optional Words:

climax	peak	emphasis	focal point

(verb)

to draw special attention to; mark with a bright color.

Optional Words:

climax	peak	point out

HILARIOUS *(adjective)*

noisily merry; extremely funny.

Optional Words:

comical	exuberant	hysterical	high-spirited
jubilant	mirthful	rollicking	riotous
lively	uproarious	amusing	sidesplitting
witty	entertaining		

HIP *(interjection)*

an exclamation used in cheering to introduce a hurrah, or give a signal for it.

(adjective slang)

well-informed or stylish.

(adjective)

aware and informed.

Optional Words:

enlightened	groovy	cool	contemporary
in-the-know	modern		

H

HISTORIC *(adjective)*

famous or important in history.

Optional Words:

celebrated	momentous	noted	prominent
renowned	significant	well-known	memorable

HOLIDAY *(noun)*

a day of festivity or recreation when no work is done.

Optional Words:

celebration	festival	fete	fiesta
respite	vacation	jubilee	feast day

HOLLER *(verb)*

to shout.

Optional Words:

bellow	clamor	yell	call
vociferate			

HOLY *(adjective)*

devoted to sacred or religious use; consecrated or sacred.

Optional Words:

blessed	celestial	divine	hallowed
righteous	sanctified	glorified	revered
worshipped	spiritual	godly	angelic
saintly	devout	moral	just
pure	perfect		

HONEST *(adjective)*

truthful and trustworthy; by fair means.

Optional Words:

candid	ethical	forthright	frank
honorable	moral	sincere	trustworthy
upright	virtuous	scrupulous	faithful
reliable	credible	gospel	factual
genuine	legitimate	licit	conscientious
valid			

(adjective)

real; straightforward.

Optional Words:

certain	factual	legitimate	correct
exact	forthright	genuine	

HONEY *(noun)*

sweetness and pleasantness; a sweet thing.

Optional Words:

dear	pet	darling	jewel

HONOR *(noun)*

great respect; high public regard; a mark of this privilege given or received; a special distinction in an examination; good personal character; a reputation for honesty and loyalty.

Optional Words:

deference	veneration	homage	reverence
admiration	esteem	devotion	acknowledgment
adulation	recognition		

H

....

HOPE *(noun)*

a feeling of expectation and desire; a desire for certain events to happen.

Optional Words:

ambition	aspiration	belief	presumption
wish	expectation	dream	

HORSEPLAY *(noun)*

boisterous play.

Optional Words:

clowning	play	joke	fooling around
fun			

HOST *(noun)*

a large number of people or things.

Optional Words:

army	legion	multitude	swarm
troop			

(noun)

a person who receives and entertains another as a guest.

Optional Words:

moderator	entertainer	emcee	hostess
master of ceremonies			

● ●

HUG *(verb)*

to squeeze tightly in one's arms; to keep close to.

Optional Words:

cling to	**cuddle**	**embrace**	**grasp**
hold	**snuggle**	**clutch**	

(noun)

a strong clasp with the arms.

Optional Words:

cling to	**cuddle**	**embrace**	**grasp**
hold	**snuggle**	**clutch**	

HUGE *(adjective)*

extremely large; enormous.

Optional Words:

giant	**grand**	**great**	**considerable**
immense	**major**	**massive**	**sizable**
towering	**vast**		

HUMOR *(noun)*

the quality of being amusing; the ability to perceive and enjoy amusement.

Optional Words:

gaiety	**joke**	**merriment**	**buffoonery**
comedy	**witticism**	**banter**	**jolliness**
gag			

HURRAH *(interjection & noun)*

an exclamation of joy or approval.

Optional Words:

hooray	**rah-rah**	**yippee**	**three cheers**
hear, hear	**hip-hip**		

● ● ● ● ● ● ● ● ● ● ● ● ● ● ● ●

H

· ·

HURRY *(noun)*

great haste; the need or desire for great haste.

Optional Words:

fleet	rush	speed

(verb)

to move or do something with haste or quickly; to cause to move in this way.

Optional Words:

bustle	dash	fly	hasten
hustle	rush	scurry	scoot
speed	dart	spur	accelerate
quicken	flit	zip	

I

Section Index

IDEAL *(adjective)*

satisfying one's idea of what is perfect; existing only in an idea; visionary.

Optional Words:
exemplary   **fitting**   **model**   **perfect**
suitable

(noun)

a person, thing or idea that is regarded as perfect or as a standard for attainment or imitation.

Optional Words:
paragon   **pattern**   **prototype**   **model**

IDOL *(noun)*

a person or thing that is the object of intense admiration or devotion.

Optional Words:
god   **icon**   **graven image**

ILLUMINATE *(verb)*

to light up; to make bright; to decorate with lights.

Optional Words:
brighten   **irradiate**   **lighten**

(verb)

to make understandable.

Optional Words:
clarify   **explain**   **illustrate**   **elucidate**

I

ILLUSTRIOUS *(adjective)*

famous and distinguished.

Optional Words:

acclaimed   **brilliant**   **celebrated**   **glorious**
magnificent   **prominent**   **renowned**

IMAGE *(noun)*

the general impression of a person, firm or product as perceived by the public.

Optional Words:

conception   **notion**   **position**   **reputation**
status

IMAGINE *(verb)*

to form a mental image of; to picture in one's mind; to think or believe; to suppose or guess.

Optional Words:

assume   **conceive**   **envisage**   **envision**
gather   **picture**   **presume**   **pretend**
suppose   **visualize**

IMMACULATE *(adjective)*

spotlessly clean.

Optional Words:

pristine   **impeccable**   **tidy**

(adjective)
free from blemish.

Optional Words:

chaste   **pristine**   **pure**   **vestal**
innocent

IMMEDIATE *(adjective)*

occurring or done at once; without delay.

Optional Words:

instant   sudden   prompt   instantaneous

IMMENSE *(adjective)*

very great in size or degree; extreme.

Optional Words:

extensive   vast   measureless

IMMERSE *(verb)*

to absorb or involve deeply in thought or business.

Optional Words:

engross   plunge   preoccupy   submerge

IMMINENT *(adjective)*

of events about to occur; likely to occur at any moment.

Optional Words:

approaching impending   near   pending

IMMORTAL *(adjective)*

famous for all time.

Optional Words:
celebrated   **divine**   **glorified**   **honored**
lauded

(adjective)
living or lasting forever; lasting a long time.

Optional Words:
eternal   **everlasting**

IMPART *(verb)*

to give.

Optional Words:
bestow   **confer**   **consign**   **entrust**
pass on   **share**

(verb)
to reveal or make known.

Optional Words:
disclose   **divulge**   **share**   **tell**

IMPARTIAL *(adjective)*

favoring all equally.

Optional Words:
neutral   **objective**   **equitable**   **just**
objective   **fair**

IMPASSIONED *(adjective)*

full of deep feeling.

Optional Words:

ardent	eager	fervent	intense
passionate	zealous		

IMPEL *(verb)*

to urge or drive to do something; to propel or drive forward.

Optional Words:

compel	constrain	force	induce
motivate	move	persuade	pressure
thrust			

IMPERATIVE *(adjective)*

essential; obligatory.

Optional Words:

compulsory	critical	mandatory	necessary
pressing	urgent		

IMPERIAL *(adjective)*

majestic; possessing commanding power or dignity; predominant.

Optional Words:

grand	kingly	lofty	queenly
regal	royal	stately	

I

IMPLEMENT *(verb)*

to put into effect; to accomplish.

Optional Words:

achieve	activate	effect	execute
fulfill	realize	start	set in motion
complete	perform		

IMPLORE *(verb)*

to request earnestly.

Optional Words:

appeal	beg	beseech	entreat
plead			

IMPORTANT *(adjective)*

having or able to have a great effect; of a person having great authority or influence.

Optional Words:

eminent	influential	major	meaningful
momentous	notable	great	consequential
prominent	vital	notable	considerable
outstanding	weighty	significant	distinguished
marked	noteworthy	worthy	conspicuous
exalted	illustrious	famed	preeminent
remarkable	worthwhile	valuable	

IMPOSING *(adjective)*

adopted to making an impression.

Optional Words:

dignified	grand	majestic	massive
stately	striking	towering	monumental

IMPRESARIO *(noun)*

an organizer of public entertainment; the manager of an operatic or concert company.

Optional Words:
producer   director

IMPRESS *(verb)*

to make a person form a strong opinion (usually favorable) of something; to fix firmly in the mind.

Optional Words:

affect	**engrave**	**establish**	**imprint**
influence	**instill**	**persuade**	**sway**
strike	**fascinate**	**inspire**	**engage**
attention	**excite**	**talk into**	**direct**
channel	**compel**	**impel**	**cajole**
convince	**move**		

IMPRINT *(verb)*

to establish firmly in the mind.

Optional Words:
memorize   impress

IMPROVE *(verb)*

to make or become better; to make an addition or alternation that improves something or adds to its value.

Optional Words:

better	**cultivate**	**enhance**	**enrich**
help	**upgrade**	**edify**	**uplift**
grow	**advance**	**prosper**	**perfect**
amend	**enhance**	**refine**	**progress**

I

INALIENABLE *(adjective)*
ability to keep.
Optional Words:
absolute   inherent

INCENTIVE *(noun)*
something that rouses or encourages a person to some action or effort.
Optional Words:

catalyst	**impetus**	**enticement**	**encouragement**
inducement	**motivation**	**stimulus**	**inspiration**
persuasion	**stimulation**	**instigation**	**incitement**

INCISIVE *(adjective)*
clear and decisive.
Optional Words:

astute	**keen**	**penetrating**	**perceptive**
probing	**trenchant**		

INCITE *(verb)*
to urge on to action; to stir up.
Optional Words:

arouse	**excite**	**induce**	**inspire**
instigate	**motivate**	**rouse**	**stimulate**

INCOMPARABLE *(adjective)*

without an equal; beyond comparison.

Optional Words:

exceptional	inimitable	matchless	peerless
singular	superior	unique	unparalleled
unrivaled			

INCORPORATE *(verb)*

to include as a part.

Optional Words:

affiliate	assimilate	comprise	consolidate
embody	exemplify	include	merge
unite			

INCREASE *(verb)*

to make or become greater in size, amount or intensity.

Optional Words:

augment	boost	elevate	enlarge
escalate	expand	multiply	raise
swell	amplify	flourish	grow
gain	evolve		

INDEED *(adverb)*

truly; really.

Optional Words:

certainly	positively	truly	actually
truthfully	sincerely	absolutely	veritably

(interjection)
used to express surprise or contempt.

I

INDEPENDENT *(adjective)*

self-governing; having one's own ideas.

Optional Words:

free　　　　**self-reliant**　　**separate**　　　**self-sufficient**
sovereign　　**autonomous**

IN-DEPTH *(adjective)*

thorough; very detailed.

Optional Words:

extensive　　**penetrating**　**profound**

INDICATE *(verb)*

to point out; to make known; to be a sign of; to show the presence of; to state briefly.

Optional Words:

display　　　　**exhibit**　　　**manifest**　　**demonstrate**

INDUCE *(verb)*

to persuade; to produce or cause.

Optional Words:

bring on　　　**coax**　　　**convince**　　**encourage**
influence　　**reason**

INDUCT *(verb)*

to install ceremonially into a benefice.

Optional Words:

admit	appoint	conscript	draft
enlist	enroll	inaugurate	initiate

INDULGE *(verb)*

to allow a person to have what he or she wishes; to gratify.

Optional Words:

cater to	coddle	favor	gratify
humor	oblige	pamper	splurge

INFINITE *(adjective)*

too great or too many to be measured or counted.

Optional Words:

interminable	eternal	indefinite	supertemporal
everlasting	perpetual	sempiternal	innumerable

INFIX *(verb)*

to fasten or fix in.

Optional Words:

instill	implant	entrench	embed
ingrain	lodge	root	

I

INFLATE *(verb)*

to puff up with pride; blow up.

Optional Words:

expand	amplify	dilate	distend
swell	fill	pump up	

INFLUENCE *(noun)*

the power to produce an effect; the ability to affect someone's character or beliefs or actions; a person or thing with this ability.

Optional Words:

authority	leverage	might	power
sway	persuasion		

INFORM *(verb)*

to communicate knowledge or information.

Optional Words:

acquaint	advise	apprise	notify
post	tell		

INGENIOUS *(adjective)*

clever at inventing new things or methods.

Optional Words:

astute	artful	bright	brilliant
creative	gifted	inventive	

INIMITABLE *(adjective)*

unique and incomparable.

Optional Words:
original

INITIATIVE *(noun)*

the first step in a process; the power or right to being something; the ability to initiate things; the beginning; starting to work.

Optional Words:

ambition	drive	enterprise	motivation

INJECT *(verb)*

to introduce something new.

Optional Words:

implant	infuse	insert	inspire
instill			

INNOVATE *(verb)*

to introduce a new process or way of doing things.

Optional Words:

change	invent	modernize	revolutionize
transform			

I

INNUMERABLE *(adjective)*
too many to be counted.
Optional Words:
countless   untold   numerous

INQUISITIVE *(adjective)*
eagerly seeking knowledge.
Optional Words:
**curious   eager   delving   questioning
probing**

INSERT *(verb)*
to put in, between or among.
Optional Words:
**enclose   implant   include   infuse
inject   introduce**

INSIGHT *(noun)*
the ability to perceive and understand the true nature of
something; knowledge obtained by this.
Optional Words:
intelligence wisdom   intuition   perspicacity

INSIST *(verb)*

to declare emphatically.

Optional Words:
demand   **press**   **urge**

INSPECT *(verb)*

to examine carefully or officially; to visit in order to make sure that rules and standards are being observed.

Optional Words:
investigate   **peruse**   **study**   **survey**

INSPIRE *(verb)*

to stimulate to creative or other activity; to express certain ideas; to fill with or instill a certain feeling; to communicate ideas by a divine agency.

Optional Words:
animate   **arouse**   **encourage**   **enkindle**
enliven   **hearten**   **induce**   **motivate**
rouse

INSTANT *(adjective)*

occurring immediately.

Optional Words:
immediate   **prompt**   **sudden**   **instantaneous**
split second

(noun)
an exact point of time; the present moment.

Optional Words:
existence   **current**   **contemporary**

I

INSTIGATE *(verb)*

to urge or incite; to bring about by persuasion.

Optional Words:

encourage   **excite**   **foment**   **inspire**
kindle   **prompt**

INSTILL *(verb)*

to implant (ideas, etc.) into a person's mind gradually.

Optional Words:

inculcate   **infix**   **inseminate**

INSTRUCT *(verb)*

to give instruction in; to authorize to act on one's behalf.

Optional Words:

advise   **direct**   **educate**   **enlighten**
inform   **notify**   **school**   **teach**
train   **tutor**

INSTRUCTIONAL *(adjective)*

imparting knowledge.

Optional Words:

educational   **scholastic**   **instructive**

INSTRUMENT *(noun)*

a person or object used and controlled by another to perform an action.

Optional Words:

agent   medium   tool   vehicle

INSTRUMENTAL *(adjective)*

serving as an instrument or means of doing something.

Optional Words:

effectual   essential   helpful   useful
valuable   vital

INTACT *(adjective)*

complete; sound.

Optional Words:

whole   entire

INTEGRATE *(verb)*

to combine or form a part or parts into a whole.

Optional Words:

blend   combine   consolidate mix
unite

I

INTEGRITY *(noun)*

honesty and incorruptibility; wholeness and soundness.

Optional Words:

character	decency	honesty	honor
principle	veracity		

INTELLECT *(noun)*

the mind's power of reasoning and acquiring knowledge; ability to use this power.

Optional Words:

aptitude	genius	sense	intelligence

INTEND *(verb)*

to have in mind as what one wishes to do or achieve; to plan that a thing shall be used or interpreted in a particular way.

Optional Words:

aim	expect	mean	plan
resolve	denote	design	endeavor

INTERACT *(verb)*

to have an effect upon each other.

Optional Words:

alloy	associate	blend	combine
hobnob	mingle	mix	compound
socialize	stir	interjoin	collaborate
merge	unify	join	

INTERCEDE *(verb)*

to intervene on behalf of another person or as a peace-maker.

Optional Words:
arbitrate   **mediate**   **negotiate**

INTERCHANGEABLE *(adjective)*

able to be interchanged.

Optional Words:
comparable **equivalent** **synonymous** **corresponding**

INTERCONNECT *(verb)*

to connect with each other.

Optional Words:
interjoin   **fuse**   **interlink**
anastomose

INTEREST *(noun)*

a feeling of curiosity about something; the quality of arousing such a feeling; advantage or benefit.

Optional Words:
attention   **investment**

(verb)
to arouse the interest of; to cause to take an interest in.

Optional Words:

absorb	**notice**	**excite**	**fascinate**
intrigue	**lure**	**tantalize**	**titillate**
pique	**attract**	**entice**	

I

INTERFUSE *(verb)*

to intersperse; to blend or fuse together.

Optional Words:

mix   join   combine

INTERJECT *(verb)*

to put in a remark when someone is speaking.

Optional Words:

insert   interpolate   interrupt

INTERLOCK *(verb)*

to fit into each other . especially so that parts engage.

Optional Words:

intervene   permeate   interpenetrate

INTERMINGLE *(verb)*

to mingle.

Optional Words:

associate	hobnob	socialize	combine
merge	join	unite	blend

INTERNALIZE *(verb)*

to learn; to absorb into the mind as a fact or attitude.

INTIMATE *(adjective)*

having a close acquaintance or friendship with a person.

Optional Words:

confidential   familiar   private   secret
trusted

INTREPID *(adjective)*

brave.

Optional Words:

bold   tough   valiant   courageous
daring   stalwart

INTRINSIC *(adjective)*

belonging to the basic nature of a person or thing.

Optional Words:

authentic   genuine   inborn   indigenous
inherent   innate   natural   real
true

I

INTRODUCE *(verb)*

to make a person known by name to others; to cause a person to become acquainted with a subject; to bring into use or into a system.

Optional Words:
**acquaint   familiarize   present   inaugurate
initiate**

INTUITION *(noun)*

the power of knowing or understanding something immediately without reasoning or being taught.

Optional Words:
feeling   inspiration   instinct

INVALUABLE *(adjective)*

having a value that is too great to be measured.

Optional Words:
**essential   precious   valuable   indispensable
rare   unique**

INVENT *(verb)*

to create by thought; to make or design; to construct.

Optional Words:
develop   devise   formulate   originate

INVEST *(verb)*

to use to buy stocks, shares or property in order to earn interest or bring profit for the buyer.

Optional Words:
allot   **finance**   **fund**

(verb)

to spend money, time or effort on something that will be useful.

Optional Words:
devote

(verb)

to endow with power.

Optional Words:
give   **grant**   **license**

INVESTIGATE *(verb)*

to examine something in order to discover the facts about it; to make a search or systematic inquiry.

Optional Words:
analyze   **explore**   **inquire into** **research**
study   **test**

INVESTITURE *(noun)*

the process of investing a person with rank or office; a ceremony at which the sovereign confers honors.

Optional Words:
inauguration coronation   enthronement

I

INVETERATE *(adjective)*

habitual; firmly established.

Optional Words:
**confirmed   constant   continuous   deep-rooted
established   recurrent**

INVIGORATE *(verb)*

to fill with vigor; to give strength or courage to.

Optional Words:
**energize   enliven   stimulate   strengthen
vitalize**

INVITE *(verb)*

to ask in a friendly way to come to one's house or to a
gathering; to ask a person formally to do something; to ask
for comments or suggestions.

Optional Words:
bid   request   solicit   summon

INVOCATION *(noun)*

invoking; calling upon God in prayer, as at the opening of a
service.

Optional Words:
prayer

INVOLVE *(verb)*

to contain within itself; to make necessary as a condition or result; to cause to share in an experience or effect.

Optional Words:

absorb	affect	comprise	concern
consist of	contain	engross	entail
include			

IRIDESCENT *(adjective)*

showing rainbowlike colors; the colored appearance caused by light rays striking the outer and inner surfaces of various bodies, such as clouds, oil films and water drops.

Optional Words:

colorful	multicolored	pearly	opalescent
prismatic			

IRRESISTIBLE *(adjective)*

too strong, convincing or delightful to be resisted.

Optional Words:

alluring	compelling	enticing	fascinating

J

J

J

JACKPOT *(noun)*

the accumulated stakes in various games, increasing in value until won; a major success.

Optional Words:

kitty	pool	profit	winnings

JEST *(noun)*

a joke.

Optional Words:

gag	prank	jape	quip

(verb)

to make jokes in fun; to be merry and cheerful.

Optional Words:

play	clown	quip	banter
josh	kid	rib	

JOIN *(verb)*

to put together; to fasten, unite or connect; to come together or become united with.

Optional Words:

adhere	adjoin	affix	associate
attach	combine	connect	consolidate
fasten	fuse	merge	interlace
secure	splice	unite	link
bind	couple	mix	marry
wed	weave	entwine	interlace

J

JOINT *(adjective)*

shared, held or done by two or more people together; sharing in an activity.

Optional Words:

collective	common	corporate	mutual
public	shared	united	intermutual

JOKE *(noun)*

something said or done to cause laughter.

Optional Words:

gag	jest	prank	trick
witticism			

JOLLY *(adverb)*

full of high spirits; cheerful and merry; very pleasant and delightful.

Optional Words:

happy	jocund	jolly	lively
spirited	joyful	festive	gleeful
jovial	gay	blithe	lighthearted

JOLT *(noun)*

a jolting movement or effect; a surprise or shock.

Optional Words:

blow	jar	shock	jounce
impact	bump		

JOSH *(verb slang)*

to hoax; to tease in a good-natured way.

Optional Words:

banter	kid	tease	clown around
rib	joke	fun	jest

JOY *(noun)*

a deep emotion of pleasure or gladness; a thing that causes this.

Optional Words:

bliss	cheer	delight	ecstasy
elation	exhilaration	gaiety	happiness
jubilation	enjoyment		

JUBILANT *(adjective)*

showing joy; rejoicing.

Optional Words:

delighted	ecstatic	elated	gladdened
joyful	radiant	gay	exultant
triumphant			

JUGGLE *(verb)*

to rearrange in order to achieve something.

Optional Words:

manage	handle	govern	regulate

J

JUMP *(verb)*

to move up off the ground; to move suddenly with a leap or bound.

Optional Words:

bounce	escalate	increase	pounce
raise	vault		

JUSTIFY *(verb)*

to show a person, statement or act to be right, just or reasonable; to be a good or sufficient reason for.

Optional Words:

adjust	align	excuse	explain
prove	verify	warrant	

K

Section Index

K

K

KEEN *(adjective)*

sharp; having a sharp edge or point; acute, penetrating or intense; perceiving things very distinctly.

Optional Words:

ardent	astute	bright	cutting
enthusiastic	intelligent	observant	poignant
well-honed			

KEY *(noun)*

a set of answers to problems.

Optional Words:

determinant   explanation   solution

KIND *(adjective)*

gentle and considerate in one's manner, character, appearance or conduct toward others.

Optional Words:

amiable   benign   generous   compassionate

KINGLY *(adjective)*

of, like or suitable for a king.

Optional Words:

imperial	masterful	powerful	puissant
majestic	monarchial	royal	sovereign
lordly	regal		

K

KNOW *(verb)*

to have in one's mind or memory as a result of experience, learning or information; to recognize with certainty; to be well informed.

Optional Words:

discern	grasp	identify	comprehend
perceive	recognize	remember	understand
ascertain	cognize		

KNOWLEDGE *(noun)*

understanding gained by experience.

Optional Words:

wisdom	intuition	perception	awareness
learning	intelligence		

KUDOS *(noun)*

honor and glory.

Optional Words:

compliment	tribute	felicitation	laudation
praise	accolade	commendation	

L

Section Index

LADYLIKE
LAND
LARGE
LARGESS
LAUD
LAUGH
LAUNCH
LAVISH
LEAD
LEADING
LEARN
LEEWAY
LEGITIMATE
LEISURE
LENGTHY
LENIENT
LESSON
LET
LETTERED
LEVEL
LIAISON
LIBERAL

LIBERTY
LICENSE
LIEF
LIFE
LIFT
LIGHT
LIKE
LISTEN
LIVE
LOGIC
LONG
LOT
LOVE
LOYAL
LUCID
LUCK
LUCRATIVE
LUMINARY
LURE
LUSTER
LUSTY
LUXURY

L

LADYLIKE *(adjective)*

polite and suitable for a lady.

Optional Words:

gentle	delicate	effeminate	womanly
cultured	well-bred	refined	genteel
elegant	urbane	gracious	mannerly
suave			

LAND *(verb)*

to arrive or cause to arrive at a certain place, stage or position.

Optional Words:

harbor	settle	light	dismount
disembark			

LARGE *(adjective)*

of considerable size or extent; of the larger kind.

Optional Words:

bulky	giant	enormous	voluminous
grand	great	heavy	gargantuan
important	major	massive	towering
vast	vital	husky	oversize
huge	hefty	sizable	extensive
plentiful	ample	lavish	substantial
liberal	jumbo	excessive	magnificent
big	spacious	colossal	considerable
corpulent	monstrous	tremendous	
immense	gigantic		

L

LARGESS (noun)

money or gifts generously given.

Optional Words:

liberality	bounty	gratuity	benevolence
favor	present	tip	contribution
donation			

LAUD (verb)

to praise.

Optional Words:

acclaim	celebrate	commend	compliment
congratulate	flatter	glorify	honor
praise	revere	venerate	extol
bless	magnify	panegyrize	adore
worship	eulogize	admire	

LAUGH (verb)

to make sounds and movements of the face and body that express lively amusement; to show joy.

Optional Words:

giggle	howl	roar	chortle
guffaw	sniggle	chuckle	heehaw
snicker	crow		

L

LAUNCH *(verb)*

to send forth by hurling or thrusting; to send on its course; to cause to move.

Optional Words:

catapult	impel	project	propel
push	thrust	throw	cast
fire	heave	hurl	pitch
originate	start	begin	drive
eject	fling	sling	toss

LAVISH *(adjective)*

giving or producing something in large quantities; plentiful.

Optional Words:

opulent	profuse	impressive	extravagant
gorgeous	luxurious	splendid	sumptuous
exorbitant	exuberant	lush	prodigal
grand			

(verb)
to bestow lavishly.

Optional Words:

give	offer

L

LEAD *(verb)*

to guide; to influence the actions or opinions of; to be in first place or position; to be the principal part in something; to head the group.

Optional Words:

conduct	convey	direct	entice
guide	induce	manage	persuade
pilot	reign	rule	steer
precede	show	point	squire
shepherd	supervise	route	move
usher	embark	head	shepherd
chaperone	drive	command	motivate
escort			

LEADING *(adjective)*

having priority or influence; chief; attention-getting; setting a precedence.

Optional Words:

first	basic	earliest	initial
main	preeminent	primary	front
head	prominent	noted	

LEARN *(verb)*

to gain knowledge of or skill in by study, experience or by being taught; to become aware by information or from observation.

Optional Words:

absorb	determine	discover	comprehend
grasp	master	memorize	realize
acquire	imbibe	peruse	understand
study	ascertain	unearth	reveal
locate	observe	perceive	

LEEWAY *(noun)*

a degree of freedom of action.

Optional Words:

liberty	license	latitude	margin
play	space		

LEGITIMATE *(adjective)*

in accordance with the law or rules.

Optional Words:

appropriate	correct	lawful	legal
licensed	proper	rightful	verifiable
true	sound	valid	authorized
licit	reliable	genuine	accredited
accepted	sure	certain	statutory

LEISURE *(noun)*

time that is free from work; time in which one can do as one chooses.

Optional Words:

freedom	holiday	opportunity	recess
relaxation	repose	respite	intermission

LENGTHY *(adjective)*

very long.

Optional Words:

drawn out	extensive	prolonged	prolix
extended	elongated	protracted	

L

LENIENT *(adjective)*

merciful; mild.

Optional Words:
**easygoing   indulgent   lax   sympathetic
tolerant**

LESSON *(noun)*

an example or experience by which one can learn; an instructive assignment.

Optional Words:
**assignment exercise   explanation guide
instruction lecture   drill**

LET *(verb)*

to allow to.

Optional Words:
authorize   consent to   permit   grant

LETTERED *(adjective)*

well-read; well-educated.

Optional Words:
**cultured   bookish   learned   scholarly
literate   erudite**

L

LEVEL *(noun)*

a measured height or value; position on a scale; relative position in rank, class or authority.

Optional Words:

amount	degree	elevation	quantity
stage	standing	status	

LIAISON *(noun)*

communication and cooperation between units of an organization.

Optional Words:

association   connection   contact

(noun)

a person who acts as a link or go-between.

Optional Words:

contact	go-between	mediator	intermediary
negotiator			

LIBERAL *(adjective)*

giving generously; ample; given in large amounts.

Optional Words:

abundant	extravagant	lavish	openhanded
plentiful	bountiful	ample	plenty

LIBERTY *(noun)*

freedom; the right or power to do as one chooses.

Optional Words:

sovereignty	permission	privilege	independence
liberation	opportunity	autonomy	emancipation

L

. . . .

LICENSE *(noun)*

liberty granted to do or omit an act; a permission.

Optional Words:

credential	document	entitlement	authorization
freedom	permit	privilege	sanction
warrant	commission		

LIEF *(adverb)*

gladly and willingly.

Optional Words:

freely	graciously

LIFE *(noun)*

being alive; the ability to function and grow that distinguishes animals and plants; liveliness.

Optional Words:

animation	breath	existence	passion
soul	spirit	vitality	

LIFT *(verb)*

to raise to a higher level or position; to look up.

Optional Words:

boost	elevate	heave	hoist
mount	ascend	arise	levitate

LIGHT *(noun)*

a kind of radiation; brightness.

Optional Words:

beacon	beam	blaze	brilliance
glow	ray	energy	illumination
splendor	sheen	emanation	lucency
luster	gleam	flame	resplendence
flare	lamp	glimmer	luminosity
sparkle			

LIKE *(verb)*

to find pleasant or satisfactory.

Optional Words:

admire	appreciate	enjoy	esteem
fancy	prize	prefer	regard
relish	revel	love	

LISTEN *(verb)*

to hear something by doing this; to pay attention.

Optional Words:

attend	hear	hearken	heed
monitor			

LIVE *(verb)*

to enjoy life to the fullest.

Optional Words:

prevail	experience

(verb)

to be energetic, vigorous, cheerful and full of action.

Optional Words:

relish	enjoy	savor	delight in

L

LOGIC *(noun)*

the ability to reason correctly.

Optional Words:

judgment	sense	wisdom	reasoning
dialectic	inference	deduction	syllogism

LONG *(adjective)*

having great length in space or time.

Optional Words:

elongated	extended	lengthy	outstretched
enlarged	expanded	protracted	continued
lasting	lingering		

(adjective)
having much of a certain quality.

Optional Words:
great

LOT *(noun)*

a large number or amount.

Optional Words:

abundance	number	heap	mass
bunch	cluster		

LOVE *(noun)*

warm liking or affection for a person; affectionate devotion.

Optional Words:

adoration	admiration	amour	devotion
esteem	infatuation	passion	regard
respect	affection	yearning	zeal
fondness	fancy	friendship	

(verb)

to be filled with delight, beauty and attractiveness, and to show it.

Optional Words:

care	cherish

LOYAL *(adjective)*

steadfast in one's allegiance to a person, cause or one's country.

Optional Words:

dedicated	dependable	devoted	devout
faithful	true	committed	firm
allegiant	ardent	constant	resolute
steadfast			

LUCID *(adjective)*

clearly expressed; easy to understand.

Optional Words:

explicit	plain	rational	understandable
translucent	transparent	fathomable	comprehensible
luminous	clear	intelligible	knowable
pellucid	graspable		

L

LUCK *(noun)*

chance; thought of as a force that brings good fortune.

Optional Words:

destiny	fate	godsend	fortuity
opportunity	windfall	advantage	kismet
triumph	karma	fluke	hap
chance	weal		

LUCRATIVE *(adjective)*

profitable; producing much money.

Optional Words:

gainful	prosperous	productive	remunerative
well-paying	worthwhile	fruitful	moneymaking
advantageous			

LUMINARY *(noun)*

a natural light-giving body, especially the sun or moon.

Optional Words:

star	sun	radiance	celestial body
light			

(noun)

an eminent or influential person.

Optional Words:

celebrity	dignitary	notable	notability
somebody			

LURE *(noun)*

something that attracts, entices or allures; its power of attracting.

Optional Words:

bait	enticement	charm	enchantment
appeal	seduction	come-on	attractiveness
inducement			

LUSTER *(noun)*

the soft brightness of a smooth or shining surface.

Optional Words:

sheen	gloss

LUSTY *(adjective)*

strong and vigorous; full of vitality.

Optional Words:

energetic	healthy	hearty	robust
dynamic	red-blooded	strenuous	vital

LUXURY *(noun)*

something costly that is enjoyable but not essential; great enjoyment or comfort.

Optional Words:

elegance	excess	frill	extravagance
indulgence	lavishness	richness	expensiveness
style	costliness		

M

M

M

M

MAGIC *(noun)*

the supposed art of controlling events or effects; an agency that works with wonderful effects.

Optional Words:
wizardry   mystic   charm   illusionary
conjury

MAGNATE *(noun)*

a wealthy and influential person, especially in business.

Optional Words:
baron   industrialist   mogul   tycoon king
capitalist   notable   personage

MAGNET *(noun)*

a person or thing that exerts a powerful attraction and charm.

Optional Words:
appeal   charisma

MAGNIFICENT *(adjective)*

splendid in appearance; excellent in quality.

Optional Words:
glorious   grand   splendid   extraordinary
superb   wonderful   majestic   proud
gorgeous   great   sublime   resplendent
exalted

M

MAGNIFY *(verb)*

to exaggerate; to overclaim the largeness, size and importance.

Optional Words:

acclaim	amplify	dramatize	enlarge
expand	glorify	increase	aggrandize
enhance	maximize	augment	

MAIN *(adjective)*

principal; most important; greatest in size or extent.

Optional Words:

chief	dominant	foremost	leading
primary	basic	fundamental	initial
preeminent	foremost	capital	

MAINTAIN *(verb)*

to cause to continue; to keep in existence.

Optional Words:

conserve	preserve	repair	secure
sustain	save		

MAJESTIC *(adjective)*

stately and dignified; imposing with sovereign power.

Optional Words:

dignified	exalted	grand	imperial
noble	regal	royal	sublime
kingly	magnificent		

MAJOR *(adjective)*

greater or very important.

Optional Words:

essential	leading	necessary	indispensable
predominant	primary	principal	significant
capital	outstanding	superior	stellar
higher	larger	upper	

(adjective)

a great part of a group or class.

Optional Words:

chief	star

MAKE *(verb)*

to construct; create or prepare from parts or from other substances; to cause to exist.

Optional Words:

build	devise	effect	fabricate
fashion	generate	create	manufacture
invent	produce		

MANAGE *(verb)*

to have under effective control; to succeed in doing or producing something.

Optional Words:

administer	control	direct	engineer
fare	handle	maneuver	oversee
superintend	lead	instruct	guide
pilot	steer	minister	council
preside			

M

MANAGER *(noun)*

a person who is in charge of the affairs of a business.

Optional Words:

boss	director	foreman	administrator
overseer	supervisor	producer	handler
impresario	executive		

MANDATE *(noun)*

authority given to someone to perform a certain task or apply certain policies.

Optional Words:

bidding	charge	commission

(verb)

to give authority to.

Optional Words:

authorize	charge	commission	direct
legislate			

MANUFACTURE *(verb)*

to make or produce (goods) on a large scale; to invent.

Optional Words:

build	concoct	construct	fabricate
forge	form	invent	make
produce	shape	carve	mold
cast	frame	execute	accomplish

MARCH *(verb)*

to walk purposefully; to progress steadily.

Optional Words:

file	parade	prance	step
stride			

M

MARKET *(noun)*

the conditions, area or opportunity for buying or selling.

(noun)
a place where goods may be sold.
Optional Words:

mart   shop   marketplace

MASS *(noun)*

a large quantity or heap.
Optional Words:

body	bulk	chunk	accumulation
collection	company	hunk	lump
mound	pile	stack	crowd

(verb)
to gather or assemble into a mass.
Optional Words:

crowd   stack

MASTER *(noun)*

someone who has complete control of people or things.
Optional Words:

authority	chief	director	principal
educator	expert	genius	lord
maestro	overlord	ruler	sage
teacher	captain	commander	head

(verb)
to overcome or bring under control; to acquire knowledge or skill in.
Optional Words:

subdue   direct   conquer   comprehend

M

MASTER OF CEREMONIES *(noun)*

a person in charge of a social or other occasion, who introduces the events or performers.

Optional Words:
reveller   emcee   master of revels

MATCH *(noun)*

a contest in a game or sport.

Optional Words:
competition   game   meet   tournament

(verb)
to put or bring together as corresponding.

Optional Words:
double   duplicate   equal

MATE *(noun)*

a fellow member or sharer; social friend.

Optional Words:
associate   colleague   companion   complement
counterpart consort   friend   match
partner   spouse

MATERIAL *(noun)*

facts, information or events to be used in composing something.

Optional Words:
data   element   figures   matter

MATURE *(adjective)*

having reached full growth or development.

Optional Words:

adult	developed	experienced	knowledgeable
grown	versed		

MAXIM *(noun)*

a general truth or rule of conduct.

Optional Words:

aphorism	cliché	epigram	platitude
proverb	saying	truism	

MAXIMUM *(noun)*

the greatest or greatest possible number, amount or intensity.

Optional Words:

apex	ceiling	climax	limit
optimum	paramount	pinnacle	summit
top	utmost		

(adjective)

greatest or greatest possible.

Optional Words:

foremost	optimum	paramount	supreme
top	utmost		

MEANING *(adjective)*

full of meaning; expressive or significant.

Optional Words:

explicit	important	profound	purposeful
significant	substantial	useful	worthwhile

M

MEANS *(plural noun)*

resources; money or other wealth considered as a means of supporting oneself.

Optional Words:

formula	fortune	method	mode
riches	wealth		

MEMORABLE *(adjective)*

worth remembering; easy to remember.

Optional Words:

impressive	monumental	notable	extraordinary
outstanding	striking	remarkable	unusual
eventful	interesting	singular	distinguished
significant	momentous	surpassing	famous
great			

MEMORIAL *(noun)*

an object, institution or custom established in memory of an event or person.

Optional Words:

marker	observance	obelisk	commemoration
plaque	shrine	statue	remembrance
testimonial			

MEND *(verb)*

to make whole or repair; to make or become better.

Optional Words:

correct	improve	patch	ready
recondition	heal	fix	reconstruct
aid	remedy	regenerate	rectify
doctor			

MERIT *(noun)*

the quality of deserving to be praised; a feature or quality that deserves praise.

Optional Words:

caliber	excellence	virtue	worth
worthiness	credit	honor	

MERRY *(adjective)*

cheerful and lively; joyous.

Optional Words:

gleeful	happy	jocular	jolly
joyful	mirthful	enjoyable	amusing
festive	blithe	gay	

MESSAGE *(noun)*

a spoken or written communication.

Optional Words:

bulletin	notice	point	memorandum
directive	dispatch	report	communiqué
memo	epistle	note	missive
broadcast			

METICULOUS *(adjective)*

giving or showing great attention to detail; very careful and exact.

Optional Words:

fastidious	particular	precise	painstaking
scrupulous	heedful	strict	conscientious
accurate			

M

MIGHT *(noun)*

great strength or power held by a person or group.

Optional Words:

authority	brawn	influence	potency
prowess	strength	sway	command
control	ability		

MILLIONAIRE *(noun)*

a person who is extremely wealthy.

Optional Words:

capitalist	tycoon	Midas

MIRACLE *(noun)*

a remarkable and welcome event that seems impossible to explain by means of the known laws of nature, and which is therefore attributed to a supernatural agency.

Optional Words:

curiosity	marvel	wonder	revelation

MODERN *(adjective)*

of the present or recent times.

Optional Words:

current	novel	new	newfangled
later	fresh	neoteric	contemporary
stylish	modish	chic	swank
prevailing	faddish	advanced	mod
contemporaneous			

MODEST (adjective)

shy about one's merits or achievements.

Optional Words:

bashful	chaste	demure	constrained
discreet	humble	meek	self-conscious
reserved			

MODIFY (verb)

to make less severe; to regulate.

Optional Words:

adjust	alter	change	control
moderate	modulate	revise	temper
vary	remodel	mutate	refashion
transform			

MOMENTOUS (adjective)

of great importance; weighty.

Optional Words:

pivotal	significant	considerable consequential
meaningful	substantial	

MOMENTUM (noun)

impetus gained by movement.

Optional Words:

drive	energy	force	impulse
thrust			

M

MONOPOLY *(noun)*

sole possession or control of anything.

Optional Words:

corner	merger	ownership	impropriation

MORALITY *(noun)*

being moral; conforming to moral principles; goodness or rightness.

Optional Words:

ethics	honesty	probity	scruples
standards	virtue	purity	righteousness
rectitude			

MOST *(adjective)*

greatest in quantity or intensity.

Optional Words:

bettermost	greater	highest	maximum
utmost	super	better	best
main	chief	primary	usual
extreme			

MOTION *(noun)*

moving; change of position; manner of movement.

Optional Words:

action	flux	mobility	motility

MOTIVATED *(adjective)*

having a definite incentive and positive desire to do things.

Optional Words:

activated	encouraged	influenced	inspired
prompted	stimulated	excited	galvanized
moved	piqued	quickened	roused
incited			

MOTTO *(noun)*

a short sentence or phrase adopted as a rule of conduct or as expressing the aims and ideals of a family, country or institution.

Optional Words:

aphorism	proverb	credo	catch phrase
maxim	principle	rule	saying
slogan	truism	adage	epigram

MOUNT *(verb)*

to ascend or go upwards; to rise to a higher level; to increase in amount, total or intensity.

Optional Words:

clamber	climb	increase	multiply
rise			

(verb)

to take action to effect.

Optional Words:

display	exhibit	install	place
position	show		

M

MOVE *(verb)*

to change or cause to change in position, place or posture; to be or cause to be in motion.

Optional Words:

affect	budge	drive	maneuver
migrate	propel	shift	stir
transfer			

(verb)
to change one's place of residence.

Optional Words:
migrate

(verb)
to make progress.

Optional Words:

influence	actuate	impel

(verb)
to provoke a reaction or emotion.

Optional Words:

affect	arouse	touch	influence
instigate	quicken	inspirit	rouse
motivate			

MUCH *(adjective)*

existing in great quantity.

Optional Words:

abundant	ample	great	considerable
large	substantial		

M

MULTIPLE *(adjective)*

having several or many parts, elements or components; having a great variety or number of things or people.

Optional Words:

profuse	plentiful	plenty	lavish
generous	great deal	heap	mass

MUNIFICENT *(adjective)*

splendidly generous.

Optional Words:

beneficent	extravagant	lavish	magnanimous
bounteous	liberal	kind	philanthropic
charitable			

MUSICAL *(adjective)*

fond of or skilled in music.

Optional Words:

euphonious	harmonious	lyrical	melodic
melodious	tuneful	songful	symphonious

MUST *(verb)*

used to express necessity or obligation; conviction of certainty.

Optional Words:

should	committal	compelled to

(noun)

anything that is required or vital.

Optional Words:

essential	duty	need	requirement

N

N

N

NAME *(verb)*

to nominate or appoint to an office.

Optional Words:

appoint	christen	term	commission
designate	identify	label	

NARRATE *(verb)*

to tell (a story); to give an account of.

Optional Words:

recite	rehearse	relate	render
unfold	disclose	reveal	chronicle
repeat	recount	depict	characterize
delineate	portray	picture	paint
describe	enumerate	detail	

NATIONALISM *(noun)*

patriotic feeling, principles or efforts.

Optional Words:

patriotism	loyalty	jingoism	provincialism

NATIVE *(adjective)*

belonging to a person or thing by nature; inborn or natural.

Optional Words:

hereditary	inbred	indigenous	inherent
innate	local	national	ingrained
congenital	fundamental	inherited	

N

NATTY *(adjective)*

neat and trim; dapper.

Optional Words:

nice	orderly	tidy	well-groomed
chic	sharp	spiffy	well-dressed
spruce	clean		

NATURAL *(adjective)*

existing in or produced by nature; in accordance with the course of nature; normal.

Optional Words:

earthy	genuine	inherent	instinctive
intuitive	native	organic	rustic
wild	intrinsic	original	essential
fundamental	inborn	ingrained	innate
congenital	incarnate		

NATURALIZE *(verb)*

to admit to full citizenship of a country; to cause to appear natural.

Optional Words:

adopt	acclimate	accustom	conform

NATURE *(noun)*

the world with all its features and living things; the physical power that produces these; a kind, sort or class; a thing's essential qualities or characteristics.

Optional Words:

biosphere	character	cosmos	macrocosm
outdoors	universe	wild	wilderness
world			

. . . .

NEAR *(adverb)*

at, to or within a short distance or interval; close or related.

Optional Words:

around	close	imminent	approaching
nearby	nigh	at hand	impending
next			

NEAT *(adjective)*

simple, clean and orderly in appearance.

Optional Words:

clean	immaculate	tidy	spick-and-spac
dapper	spruce	elegant	well-groomed
trim			

(adjective)

done or doing things in a precise and skillful way.

Optional Words:

orderly	organized	methodical	regular
systematic	exact	meticulous	precise

NECESSARY *(adjective)*

essential in order to achieve something; inevitable; involved as a condition, accompaniment or result.

Optional Words:

essential	imperative	obligatory	indispensable
required	requisite	expedient	fundamental
needful	urgent	basic	imperative
pressing	vital	cardinal	significant
compulsory	paramount	compelling	

N

NEED *(noun)*

circumstances in which a thing or course of action is required; a thing necessary for life.

Optional Words:

necessity	obligation	want	requirement
exigency	compulsion		

NEW *(adjective)*

recently made, invented, discovered or experienced; different.

Optional Words:

current	faddish	fashionable	fresh
innovative	inventive	modern	novel
popular	pristine	first-hand	neoteric
recent	late	modish	latest
unique	original	primary	distinct
chic	present	vogue	contemporary
crisp	raw	young	original
novice			

NEXT *(adjective)*

living or being nearest to something; coming nearest in order.

Optional Words:

adjacent	adjoining	bordering	ensuing
following	neighboring	subsequent	succeeding
coming	consecutive		

N

NICE *(adjective)*

pleasant and satisfactory.

Optional Words:

congenial	agreeable	amicable	gratifying
excellent	friendly	marvelous	pleasurable
virtuous	winning	winsome	refined
charming	inviting	cordial	courteous
ingratiating	gracious	becoming	fine
considerate	genial	kind	gentle
demure	kindly	seemly	delicate
decorous	proper	modest	good
decent	favorable		

(adjective)

a subtle distinction or detail.

Optional Words:

exact	precise	discerning

NICHE *(noun)*

a position in life or employment to which the holder is well suited.

Optional Words:

cranny	corner	cubbyhole	recess

NIMBLE *(adjective)*

able to move quickly; agile.

Optional Words:

adroit	deft	dexterous	sprightly
spry	graceful	active	brisk
lithesome			

N

NOBLE *(adjective)*

belonging to the aristocracy by birth or rank.

Optional Words:

aristocratic	patrician	princely	blue-blooded
royal			

(adjective)

possessing excellent qualities, especially character.

Optional Words:

admirable	estimable	grand	majestic
stately	virtuous	reputable	magnanimous
courtly	splendid	supreme	lordly
dignified	sublime	valuable	chivalrous
regal			

NOD *(verb)*

to move the head down and up again quickly as a sign of agreement or casual greeting; to indicate (agreement etc.) in this way.

Optional Words:

cue	motion	okay	sign
signal			

(noun)

to give or get agreement or a signal to proceed.

Optional Words:

approval	go-ahead	okay	permission
sign	signal	cue	

NOMINATE *(verb)*

to name as candidate for or future holder of an office.

Optional Words:

advocate	appoint	designate	name
propose	recommend	suggest	

NORMAL *(adjective)*

conforming to what is standard or usual.

Optional Words:

average	ordinary	regular	typical
usual	prevalent	routine	conventional
general	common	customary	natural
typical			

NOTABLE *(adjective)*

worthy of notice; remarkable; eminent.

Optional Words:

important	striking	unusual	celebrated
renowned	famous	big	distinguished
dignitary	luminary	illustrious	famed
prominent	well-known	chief	

NOTICE *(noun)*

written or printed information or instructions displayed publicly.

Optional Words:

attention	caution	information	announcement
knowledge	notification	commentary	enlightenment
declaration			

(verb)

to make something known.

Optional Words:

heed	inform	notify	declare
caution	enlighten	announce	

N

NOURISH *(verb)*

to foster or cherish.

Optional Words:

bolster	endure	feed	maintain
preserve	support	uphold	withstand
cultivate	nurture	sustain	provide

NOUS *(noun)*

common sense.

Optional Words:

good sense	wisdom	judgment	reason

NOVELTY *(noun)*

the quality of being new; a new thing or occurrence.

Optional Words:

change	freshness	newness	originality
uniqueness	fashionable	odd	

NOW *(adverb)*

at or during the present time; immediately.

Optional Words:

momentarily	promptly	forthwith	instantly
presently	directly		

(noun)

at present time, moment or occasion

Optional Words:

today	here and now

NUMEROUS *(adjective)*

many; consisting of many items.

Optional Words:

abundant	diverse	myriad	several
sundry	copious	various	infinite
legion	multifarious	populous	multitudinous
voluminous			

O

O

O

OBJECTIVE *(adjective)*

having real existence outside a person's mind.

Optional Words:

detached	impartial	extraneous	sensible
actual	external	material	determinable
sure	extrinsic	measurable	

OBLIGE *(verb)*

to help or gratify by performing a small service; to be courteous.

Optional Words:

aid	assist	indulge	accommodate
serve	gratify	please	avail
benefit	profit	help	

OBSERVANCE *(noun)*

the keeping of a law, rule or custom; the keeping or celebrating of a religious festival or of a holiday.

Optional Words:

ritual	liturgy	practice	rite
custom			

OBTAIN *(verb)*

to get; to come into possession of (a thing) by effort or as a gift.

Optional Words:

acquire	gain	grasp	procure
purchase	secure	glean	reap
receive	collect	win	gather
inherit	realize		

O

OBVIOUS *(adjective)*

easy to see, recognize or understand.

Optional Words:

apparent	clear	distinct	conspicuous
evident	intelligible	manifest	noticeable
plain	prominent	striking	perceptible
overt	glaring	evident	observable
public	visible		

OCCASION *(noun)*

the time at which a particular event takes place; a special event; a suitable time for doing something; an opportunity, need, reason or cause.

Optional Words:

break	chance	episode	circumstance
happening	incident	occurrence	opening
opportunity			

OCCUR *(verb)*

to come into being as an event or process.

Optional Words:

arise	develop	ensue	eventuate
happen			

ODDS *(plural noun)*

the probability that a certain thing will happen; this expressed as a ratio.

Optional Words:

advantage	chance	edge	disadvantage
handicap	likelihood	probability	allowance
vantage			

O

OFFER *(verb)*

to present so that it may be accepted, rejected or considered.

Optional Words:

bid   propose   submit

OFFICIATE *(verb)*

to act in an official capacity; to be in charge.

Optional Words:

conduct	direct	emcee	judge
preside	umpire	govern	manage

OFTEN *(adverb)*

frequently; many times; at short intervals; in many instances.

Optional Words:

habitually	recurrently	repeatedly	usually
oft	oftentimes		

OH *(interjection)*

an exclamation of surprise and delight, used for emphasis.

Optional Words:

indeed   good   certainly   very well

O

OK *(adverb & adjective)*
>
> all right; satisfactory.
>
> ***Optional Words:***
> **correct   yes   surely   affirmative
> agreed**
>
> *(noun)*
> approval; agreement to a plan.

OMEN *(noun)*
>
> an event regarded as a prophetic sign.
>
> ***Optional Words:***
> **forewarning harbinger   indication   portent
> premonition sign**

OMNIPOTENT *(adjective)*
>
> having great power and extensive knowledge.
>
> ***Optional Words:***
> **all-powerful almighty   sovereign   supreme**

OMNIPRESENT *(adjective)*
>
> present everywhere; ubiquitous.
>
> ***Optional Words:***
> **infinite   universal**

O

ONGOING *(adjective)*

continuing to exist or progress.

Optional Words:

constant   **continuing**   **current**   **lasting**
open-ended   **continuous**

ONRUSH *(noun)*

an onward rush.

Optional Words:

advance   **charge**   **deluge**   **flood**
rush   **wave**   **surge**

ONSET *(noun)*

a beginning.

Optional Words:

beginning   **start**   **opening**   **commencement**

ONWARD *(adverb & adjective)*

with an advancing motion; further on.

Optional Words:

ahead   **farther**   **forth**   **forward**
beyond   **alee**

O

OPEN *(adjective)*

willing to receive; not closed.

Optional Words:

accessible   agape   ajar   exposed

(verb)

to begin or establish an opportunity publicly.

Optional Words:

clear   expose

OPTIMISM *(noun)*

a tendency to take a hopeful view of things or to expect that results will be good.

Optional Words:

confidence	enthusiasm	hopefulness	idealism
positivism	expectation	anticipation	sureness
certainty	Polyannaism		

OPTIMIZE *(verb)*

to make as effective or favorable as possible.

Optional Words:

amplify	augment	expand	increase
magnify	extend		

OPTION *(noun)*

freedom to choose; a thing that is or may be chosen.

Optional Words:

alternative	choice	opportunity	possibility
privilege	right	selection	free will
preference	druthers		

OPULENT *(adjective)*

wealthy and rich; abundant; luxuriant.

Optional Words:

affluent	ample	bounteous	copious
lavish	plentiful	sumptuous	well-to-do
lush			

ORCHESTRATE *(verb)*

to compose or arrange for performance; to coordinate (things) deliberately.

Optional Words:

direct	manage	organize	plan
score	blend	integrate	unify
synthesize	symphonize		

ORDAIN *(verb)*

to appoint ceremonially to perform spiritual functions in the Christian Church; to appoint or decree authoritatively.

Optional Words:

appoint	command	commission	confer
consecrate	decree	dictate	invest
order	prescribe		

O

ORDER *(noun)*

the way in which things are placed in relation to one another; a proper or customary sequence.

Optional Words:

sequence	category	class	classification
method	progression	regularity	arrangement
shape	orderliness		

(noun)

the condition brought about by good and firm government and obedience to the laws.

Optional Words:

harmony

(noun)

a system of rules or procedure.

Optional Words:

genre	pattern	plan	society

ORGANIZE *(verb)*

to arrange in an orderly or systematic way; to make arrangements for.

Optional Words:

array	categorize	establish	institute
order	correlate	classify	setup
methodize	systemize		

ORIGINAL *(adjective)*

thinking or acting for oneself; inventive or creative.

Optional Words:

authentic	ingenious	initial	innovative
novel	incipient	neoteric	inceptive

(noun)

the first form of something; the thing from which another is copied.

Optional Words:

earliest	first	forerunner	opening
rudimentary	primitive	beginning	primary
prototype			

ORNAMENT *(verb)*

elaborately decorate or design.

Optional Words:

adorn	beautify	bedeck	deck
decorate	dress (up)	embellish	trim
embroider	gilt		

OUTCLASS *(verb)*

to surpass greatly; to exceed decisively in skill, quality or powers.

Optional Words:

outdo	excel	surpass	exceed

O

OUTDISTANCE *(verb)*

to get far ahead of; to surpass completely.

Optional Words:

exceed	beat	outpace	outstrip
outspend	outdo	outrun	

OUTGOING *(adjective)*

sociable and friendly.

Optional Words:

congenial	extroverted	friendly	demonstrative
gregarious	sociable	civil	

OUTING *(noun)*

a pleasure trip.

Optional Words:

drive	excursion	hike	jaunt
picnic	ride	trip	walk
airing	junket	sally	

OUTLANDISH *(adjective)*

looking or sounding strange or foreign.

Optional Words:

bizarre	curious	eccentric	incredible
peculiar	unusual	queer	strange
singular	odd		

OUTLOOK *(noun)*

a person's mental attitude or way of looking at something.

Optional Words:

approach	philosophy	view	vision
standpoint	slant		

(noun)
future prospects.

Optional Words:

expectation	forecast	prediction	prospect

OUTMATCH *(verb)*

to be more than.

Optional Words:

best	surpass	outgo	outshine
pass	top		

OUTRAGEOUS *(adjective)*

greatly exceeding what is moderate or reasonable.

Optional Words:

excessive	exorbitant	extreme	enormous
gross			

OUTRIGHT *(adjective)*

thorough and complete.

Optional Words:

altogether	entire	utter	absolute
downright	total	all	consummate
whole			

O

OUTRUN *(verb)*

to run faster or further than; to go beyond.

Optional Words:
outdistance   outpace   outspeed   outstrip

OUTSELL *(verb)*

to sell or be sold in greater quantities than.

Optional Words:
excel   surpass   exceed

OUTSHINE *(verb)*

to surpass in splendor or excellence.

Optional Words:
beat   best   exceed   transcend

OUTSTANDING *(adjective)*

exceptionally good.

Optional Words:
choice   excellent   exceptional   notable
prominent   renowned   striking   salient
remarkable   noticeable

OVATION *(noun)*

enthusiastic applause.

Optional Words:

acclamation	cheering	clapping	hand
hurrah	salvo	laudation	praise

OVERJOYED *(adjective)*

filled with very great joy.

Optional Words:

delighted	delirious	elated	thrilled

OWN *(verb)*

to have as one's property; to posses.

Optional Words:

have	hold	control	occupy
retain			

P

Defined Words and Synonyms
Page 346

P

P

PROFUSE
PROGRESS
PROJECT
PROJECTION
PROMINENT
PROMISE
PROMOTE
PROMPT
PROPEL
PROPER
PROPERTY
PROPHECY
PROPITIATE
PROPONENT
PROPOSE
PROPRIETARY
PROPRIETY
PROSPER
PROTECT
PROTOCOL
PROUD
PROVE
PROVIDE
PROVIDENT
PRUDENT
PUBLICITY
PUBLISH
PULL
PURCHASE
PURE
PURPOSE
PURSUANCE

P

PACIFY *(verb)*

to calm and quiet; to establish peace.

Optional Words:

soothe	temper	tranquilize	propitiate
lull	dulcify	allay	moderate
appease	conciliate	placate	smooth over

PACT *(noun)*

an agreement; a treaty.

Optional Words:

alliance	bargain	contract	covenant
settlement	compact	bond	

PAGEANT *(noun)*

a public show consisting of a procession of people in costume; an outdoor performance of a historical play.

Optional Words:

ceremony	exhibition	panorama	extravaganza
parade	spectacle	celebration	

PALATABLE *(adjective)*

pleasant to the taste or to the mind.

Optional Words:

appetizing	delectable	luscious	savory
relishing	sapid	flavorsome	delightful
tasty	delicious		

P

PALATIAL *(adjective)*

like a palace; spacious and splendid.

Optional Words:

elegant	grand	imposing	magnificent
opulent	stately	regal	deluxe
plush	luxurious	lush	

PANACHE *(noun)*

a confident, stylish manner.

Optional Words:

class	crest	distinction	magnificence
elegance	flair	grandeur	splendor
style			

PAN OUT *(verb)*

to turn out; to be successful in outcome.

Optional Words:

yield	net	work out	result
succeed	come off		

PARABLE *(noun)*

a story told to illustrate a moral or spiritual truth.

Optional Words:

allegory	fable	lesson	tale
myth			

P

PARADE (noun)

a procession of people or things, especially in a display or exhibition.

Optional Words:

cavalcade	pageant	motorcade	demonstration
spectacle	ceremony	fanfare	

PARADIGM (noun)

something serving as an example or model of how things should be done.

Optional Words:

ideal	pattern	prototype	standard
criterion	archetype		

PARADISE (noun)

heaven; the ultimate abode for righteous souls; a region or state of surpassing delight.

Optional Words:

bliss	ecstasy	Eden	Elysium
rapture	utopia		

PARAMOUNT (adjective)

having the highest title; superior to all others.

Optional Words:

chief	master	eminent	ascedant
dominant	sovereign	foremost	preeminent
principal	superior	supreme	

P

....

PARDON *(noun)*

forgiveness; kind indulgence.

Optional Words:

absolution	amnesty	clemency	grace
remission	vindication	leniency	mercy
liberation			

PAR EXCELLENCE *(adjective)*

more than all others; in the highest degree.

Optional Words:

superior	preeminent	excellent	quintessential
champion	classic	first-class	number one
prime	supreme		

PARTAKE *(verb)*

to participate; to take part of or have a special share.

Optional Words:

join in	share	receive

PARTICULAR *(adjective)*

special or exceptional; selecting carefully; insisting on certain standards.

Optional Words:

certain	definite	detailed	conscientious
exclusive	fastidious	individual	meticulous
precise	specific	thorough	unique

PARTY *(noun)*

a social gathering, usually of invited guests.

Optional Words:

affair	fete	celebration	gala
occasion	festivity	gathering	soiree

(noun)

a number of people traveling or working together as a unit; a group of people united in support of a cause or policy, especially a political group organized on a national basis to put forward its policies and candidates for office.

Optional Words:

band	faction	team	bloc
coalition			

PASS *(verb)*

to go, proceed, move onward or past something.

Optional Words:

accomplish	advance	convey	elapse
employ	enact	fulfill	legislate
occur	proceed	progress	ratify
spend	surpass		

PASSION *(noun)*

strong emotion; great enthusiasm for something; the object of great enthusiasm.

Optional Words:

affection	appetite	ardor	craving
desire	emotion	fancy	fervor
hunger	infatuation	intensity	love

P

························

PATIENT *(adjective)*

having or showing patience.

Optional Words:

enduring	forbearing	serene	steady
tranquil	calm	passive	easy-going
tolerant			

PATRON *(noun)*

a person who gives encouragement, financial or other support to an activity or cause.

Optional Words:

advocate	benefactor	champion	client
customer	sponsor	supporter	allay
backer	protector	defender	philanthropist
helper	encourager	friend	

PAY *(verb)*

to give in return for goods or services; to give what is owed; to be profitable or worthwhile; to bestow, render or express.

Optional Words:

compensate	disburse	expend	extend
grant	outlay	profit	settle
square	yield	commission	reimburse
reward			

PEACE *(noun)*

quiet and calm; a state of harmony between people.

Optional Words:

accord	composure	harmony	serenity
tranquillity	concord	contentment	

PEAK *(noun)*

the point of highest value, achievement or intensity.

Optional Words:

apex	apogee	climax	crest
crown	maximum	mountain	pinnacle
summit	vortex	zenith	height
tip			

PEAL *(noun)*

the loud ringing of a bell or set of bells; a loud burst of thunder or laughter.

Optional Words:

clap	bong	chime	knell
toll			

PEARL *(noun)*

something valued because of its excellence or beauty.

Optional Words:

gem	jewel	treasure

PEERLESS *(adjective)*

without equal; superb.

Optional Words:

matchless	unique	paramount	incomparable
only	dominant	supreme	best
perfect	excellent	superior	

P

PELLUCID *(adjective)*

very clear; permitting a passage of light to a certain extent.

Optional Words:

crystal	lucent	lucid	transparent
luminous	limpid	gauzy	translucent
simple	sheer		

PEP *(noun slang)*

vigor, energy or sprightliness.

Optional Words:

gusto	life	spirit	strength
vitality	zip	punch	snap
bang	get up	hardiness	moxie
liveliness			

PERCEPTION *(noun)*

the ability to perceive; having or showing insight and sensitive understanding; cognition of fact or truth, especially by the activity of thinking.

Optional Words:

conception	sagacity	knowledge	understanding
acumen	opinion	judgment	intellection
observation			

P

PERFECT *(adjective)*

complete or faultless; having all its essential qualities.

Optional Words:

absolute	complete	entire	consummate
exact	exemplary	ideal	impeccable
intact	pure	sheer	whole
classical	crowning	sublime	full
thorough	sharp	excellent	total

(verb)
to make perfect.

Optional Words:

accomplish   polish   purify

PERFORMANCE *(noun)*

a notable action or achievement.

Optional Words:

appearance	execution	exhibition	accomplishment
presentation	show	attainment	consummation

PERK *(verb)*

to raise (the head, etc.) briskly or jauntily; to regain or cause to regain courage, confidence or vitality; to smarten up; to be lively and cheerful.

Optional Words:

improve	revive	recuperate	invigorate
enliven			

P

PERMISSION *(noun)*

consent or authorization to do something.

Optional Words:

acquiescence	allowance	consent	authorization
endorsement	license	permit	recognition
concurrence			

PERSEVERE *(verb)*

to continue steadfastly and firmly; to continue to exist.

Optional Words:

abide	carry on	persist	endure
labor	remain	sustain	

PERSONALITY *(noun)*

a person's own distinctive character.

Optional Words:

character	demeanor	disposition	manner
nature	temperament		

(noun)

a person with distinctive qualities.

Optional Words:

celebrity	dignitary	star	personage

PERSPECTIVE *(noun)*

a mental picture of the relative importance of things.

Optional Words:

attitude	outlook	position	viewpoint
vista			

P

PERSUADE (verb)

to cause to believe or do something by reasoning with.

Optional Words:

affect	allure	coax	convert
convince	enlist	entice	induce
influence	sell	sway	assure
move	cajole		

PERT (adjective)

cheeky and lively.

Optional Words:

alert	chipper	perky	saucy
sprightly	bold	daring	

PERTINACIOUS (adjective)

holding firmly to an opinion or course of action; persistent and determined.

Optional Words:

resolute	attentive	tenacious

PETITION (noun)

an earnest request.

Optional Words:

appeal	entreaty	invocation	supplication
plea	prayer		

P

∙∙∙∙∙∙∙∙∙∙∙∙∙∙∙∙∙∙∙∙∙∙∙∙∙∙∙

PHENOMENON *(noun)*

a fact, occurrence or change perceived by any of the senses or by the mind; a remarkable person or thing; something extraordinary and remarkable.

Optional Words:

curiosity	event	happening	incident
marvel	sensation	wonder	prodigy
appearance	stunner		

PHILANTHROPIC *(adjective)*

benevolent; concerned with human welfare and the reduction of suffering; loving of mankind.

Optional Words:

altruistic	charitable	generous	magnanimous
munificent	good	humane	humanitarian

PICNIC *(noun)*

something very agreeable or easily done.

Optional Words:

breeze	snap	cinch	duck soup
child's play	pie	joy ride	sure thing
cakewalk			

(noun)
an outdoor party, usually held in the countryside, during which a meal is eaten.

PICTURESQUE *(adjective)*

forming a striking and pleasant scene; very expressive and vivid.

Optional Words:

artistic	attractive	charming	colorful
delightful	pictorial	scenic	graphic
arresting	pretty	unusual	

PIQUANT *(adjective)*

pleasantly sharp in its taste or smell; pleasantly stimulating or exciting to the mind.

Optional Words:

interesting	lively	pungent	spirited
vigorous	zesty	enticing	exciting
charming	sparkling		

PIZZAZZ *(noun)*

zest and liveliness; unusual panache.

Optional Words:

kick	pungency	punch	flamboyant
snap	flashy	brilliant	scintillating
ginger			

PLACID *(adjective)*

calm and peaceful.

Optional Words:

still	rest	serene	repose
quiet			

P

· ·

PLAN *(verb)*

to make a plan or design of; to arrange a method.

Optional Words:

aim	arrange	chart	design
devise	intend	map-out	order
organize	outline	prepare	propose

(noun)

a method for doing something.

pattern	strategy	diagram	blueprint
design	sketch	mission	

PLANT *(verb)*

to fix, set or place in position.

Optional Words:

inlay	insert	inset	instill
sow	pot	stock	establish

PLATITUDE *(noun)*

a commonplace remark, especially one uttered solemnly as if it were new.

Optional Words:

banality	cliché	proverb	triviality
motto	truism		

PLAUSIBLE *(adjective)*

seeming to be reasonable or probable but not proved.

Optional Words:

believable	credible	feasible	likely
logical	possible	sound	supposable

PLAY *(verb)*

to occupy oneself in a game or other recreational activity; to take part in.

Optional Words:

act	caper	sport	delight
dally	frolic	romp	

(noun)

activity or operation; free movement.

Optional Words:

act	comedy	sport	amusement
fun	recreation	diversion	entertainment
gambol	delight	enjoyment	

PLEASE *(verb)*

to give pleasure to; to make one feel satisfied or glad; to feel joy; a source of pleasure.

Optional Words:

charm	delight	desire	gladden
gratify	like	satisfy	suit
thrill			

PLEDGE *(noun)*

a solemn promise.

Optional Words:

compact	covenant	oath	vow
word	warrant		

P

PLUSH *(adjective)*

luxurious.

Optional Words:

elegant	lavish	opulent	posh
sumptuous	rich	deluxe	luscious
palatial			

POETRY *(noun)*

a quality that pleases the mind as poetry does; the art by which the poet projects feelings and experience onto an imaginative plane; rhythmical words to stir emotions.

Optional Words:

verse	poem	song	versification
rime	rhyme	stanza	poesy

POISE *(verb)*

to balance or be balanced.

Optional Words:

balance	float	hang	hover
perch	stabilize	stand	support

(noun)

a dignified and self-assured manner.

Optional Words:

balance	composure	confidence	dignity
equilibrium	grace	gravity	

P

POLICY *(noun)*

the course or general plan of action adopted by a government, party or person.

Optional Words:

design	method	practice	procedure
routine	strategy	style	system
tenent	doctrine	theory	administration
tactic			

POLISH *(noun)*

a high degree of elegance; refined or perfect.

Optional Words:

breeding	culture	elegance	luster
poise	refinement		

POLITE *(adjective)*

having good manners; socially correct and refined.

Optional Words:

chivalrous	considerate	cordial	courteous
courtly	cultured	gallant	genteel
mannerly	polished	respectful	tactful
obliging	thoughtful	concerned	affable
attentive	pleasant	agreeable	

POLITIC *(adjective)*

sagacious in planning; artful, especially in planning.

Optional Words:

decorous	delicate	diplomatic	discreet
judicious	polite	thoughtful	

P

POMP *(noun)*

stately and splendid; ceremonial.

Optional Words:

affectation	ceremony	display	exhibition
pageantry	splendor	magnificence	

PONDER *(verb)*

to be deep in thought; to think something over thoroughly; to think with an appreciable weight or significance.

Optional Words:

consider	meditate	muse	contemplate
reflect	think	deliberate	mind
perpend	study	evaluate	weigh
appraise			

POP *(noun)*

a small explosive sound.

Optional Words:

bang	burst	crack

(verb)

to come or go quickly, suddenly or unexpectedly.

Optional Words:

appear	bang	burst	crack
explode	materialize	dart	leap
jump			

P

POPULAR *(adjective)*

liked or enjoyed by many people; a belief held by many people.

Optional Words:

accepted	approved	celebrated	common
current	famous	fashionable	favored
preferred	prevalent	renowned	well-liked
favorite	attractive	pleasing	leading
suitable	noted	lovable	

POSITIVE *(adjective)*

expressed clearly and usually peremptorily.

Optional Words:

categorical	decided	definite	decisive
specific	complete	affirmative	sure
certain	explicit	firm	factual
absolute			

POSITIVELY *(adverb)*

definitely.

Optional Words:

certainly	precisely	genuinely	ultimately
ideally	infinitely	utterly	transcendentally
grossly	clearly	strictly	peremptorily
absolutely	assertively	decidedly	authoritatively
exactly	accurately	specifically	thoroughly
expressly	obviously	plainly	conclusively
simply			

P

POSSESS (verb)

to have as property.

Optional Words:

own	have	control	maintain
hold	occupy	retain	

POWERFUL (adjective)

having or manifesting power to effect great or striking results; energetic strength; in control, influential and authoritative.

Optional Words:

capable	intense	forceful	commanding
mighty	omnipotent	potent	puissant
competent	effectual	dynamic	vigorous
masterful	sturdy	zealous	spirited
exuberant	driving	vibrant	strong
able	strenuous	dominant	tough
stout	masterful	effective	authoritative

PRAISE (verb)

to show approval of.

Optional Words:

award	endorse	aggrandize	admire
cajole	hail	acclaim	recommend
greet	honor	salute	commend
cheer	glorify	exalt	compliment
celebrate	extol	eulogize	adore
bless	flatter	laud	panegyrize
ennoble	plug	revere	hallow
worship	sanctify	venerate	

P

PREDICT *(verb)*

to forecast; to prophesy.

Optional Words:

anticipate	calculate	divine	estimate
foresee	foretell	guess	foreshadow
speculate	theorize		

PREEMINENT *(adjective)*

excelling others; outstanding.

Optional Words:

celebrated	eminent	consummate	distinguished
famous	foremost	greatest	predominant
renowned	unparalleled	unrivaled	

PREFER *(verb)*

to choose as more desirable; to favor; to hold in higher regard or esteem.

Optional Words:

elect	opt	pick	select
single	promote	fancy	

PREMIER *(adjective)*

first in importance, order or time.

Optional Words:

chief	foremost	main	primary
principal	champion	arch	head
leading			

P

PREPOSSESSING *(adjective)*

attractive; making a good impression from the beginning.

Optional Words:

alluring	appealing	captivating	charming
enchanting	engaging	handsome	pleasant

PRESCRIPT *(noun)*

a law, rule or command.

Optional Words:

decree	edict	ordinance	regulation
precept			

PRESENCE *(noun)*

a person's bearing; impressiveness of bearing.

Optional Words:

appearance	attendance	carriage	composure
conduct	demeanor	poise	refinement

PRESENT *(verb)*

to give as a gift or award; to offer for acceptance; to introduce to another or others; to show or reveal.

Optional Words:

accord	confer	contribute	demonstrate
display	donate	offer	tender

P

PRESERVE *(verb)*

to keep safe; to keep in an unchanged condition.

Optional Words:

conserve	harbor	maintain	perpetuate
reserve	safeguard	save	shelter
shield	spare	sustain	uphold

PRESIDENT *(noun)*

a person who is the head of a club, society or council; the head of a republic.

Optional Words:

chair	chief	commander	administrator
head	ruler	executive	presiding officer

PRESTIGE *(noun)*

respect for a person resulting from his or her good reputation, past achievements, etc.

Optional Words:

authority	celebrity	dignity	distinction
eminence	influence	power	illustriousness
renown	stature	status	prominence
sway	fame		

PRETTY *(adjective)*

attractive in a delicate way.

Optional Words:

beautiful	bonny	comely	good-looking
delightful	fair	gorgeous	handsome
lovely	nice	pleasant	pleasing
cute	winsome		

P

PREVAIL *(verb)*

to be victorious; to gain the mastery.

Optional Words:

abound	conquer	influence	predominate
persuade	control	succeed	preponderate
triumph	win		

PREVALENT *(adjective)*

existing or occurring, generally widespread.

Optional Words:

general	predominant	usual

PRICELESS *(adjective)*

beyond price or valuation.

Optional Words:

costly	expensive	inestimable	precious
invaluable			

PRIME *(adjective)*

chief or most important; first-rate or excellent.

Optional Words:

choice	elite	excellent	leading
paramount	principal	quality	top
first-class	superior	capital	famous

(adjective)

basic or fundamental.

Optional Words:

principal	first	earliest	initial

P

PRINCELY *(adjective)*

splendid and generous.

Optional Words:

magnificent	royal	stately	august
baronial	lordly	noble	grand

PRINCIPAL *(adjective)*

first in rank or importance.

Optional Words:

cardinal	chief	head	main
major	paramount	primary	ruling
ultimate			

(noun)

the person with highest authority in an organization.

Optional Words:

chief	dean	head	headmaster
major	proctor	rector	superintendent

PRINCIPLE *(noun)*

a basic truth; a general law or doctrine that is used as a basis of reasoning or a guide to action or behavior; a personal code of right conduct.

Optional Words:

axiom	belief	creed	ethics
integrity	morality	motive	precept
rationale	reason	regulation	rule
standards			

P

PRIORITY *(noun)*

being earlier or more important; precedence in rank; the right to be first; something that is more important than other items or considerations.

Optional Words:

preference	rank	seniority	preeminence
tenure	superiority	antecendence	

PRIVILEGE *(noun)*

a special right or advantage granted to one person or group.

Optional Words:

advantage	entitlement	due	carte blanche
liberty	license	birthright	allowance
appanage	favor		

PRIZE *(noun)*

an award given as a symbol of victory or superiority.

Optional Words:

gem	jewel	medallion	endowment
reward	ribbon	treasure	trophy
laurel	crown	citation	championship
title	bonus	bounty	

PROBABLE *(adjective)*

likely to happen or be true.

Optional Words:

conceivable	feasible	likely	presumable
reasonable	possible	believable	credible
plausible			

P

PROBITY *(noun)*

honesty and integrity.

Optional Words:

character	decency	honor	principle
goodness	morality	virtue	righteousness
uprightness			

PROCLAIM *(verb)*

to announce officially or publicly; to declare.

Optional Words:

blazon	broadcast	decree	herald
ordain	pronounce		

PROCURE *(verb)*

to obtain by care or effort; to acquire.

Optional Words:

capture	gain	grasp	purchase
secure	seize	get	annex
have	land		

PRODIGY *(noun)*

a person with exceptional qualities or abilities; a marvelous thing; a wonderful example of something.

Optional Words:

genius	marvel	sensation	phenomenon
wonder	stunner	miracle	spectacle
curiosity			

P

PRODUCE *(verb)*

to bring forward for inspection, consideration or use; to bring into existence; to cause a reaction or sensation; to manufacture.

Optional Words:

accomplish	assemble	compose	construct
create	effect	furnish	generate
make	manifest	propagate	provide
show	yield	bear	fabricate
erect	form	reproduce	proliferate

PROFESS *(verb)*

to state that one has a quality or feeling; to pretend; to affirm one's faith in.

Optional Words:

allege	aver	avouch	claim
declare	pronounce	purport	

PROFESSION *(noun)*

an occupation, especially one that involves knowledge and training in a branch of advanced learning.

Optional Words:

career	craft	livelihood	specialty
lifework	business	billet	avocation
service	skill	pursuit	engagement
field	calling	position	sphere

PROFICIENT *(adjective)*

doing something correctly and competently through training or practice.

Optional Words:

able	adept	capable	competent
masterful	skillful	expert	

PROFIT *(noun)*

an advantage or benefit obtained from doing something.

Optional Words:

gain	improvement

(noun)

money gained in a business.

Optional Words:

earnings	proceeds	returns	revenue
receipts	remuneration		

PROFITABLE *(adjective)*

bringing profit or gain.

Optional Words:

favorable	lucrative	propitious	remunerative
well-paying	worthwhile	worthy	advantageous
beneficial	valuable	desirable	expedient
productive	useful	prosperous	helpful

P

PROFOUND *(adjective)*

deep or intense; having or showing great knowledge of or insight into a subject.

Optional Words:

acute	enigmatic	erudite	consequential
extreme	heartfelt	important	penetrating
sage	serious	significant	philosophical
wise			

PROFUSE *(adjective)*

lavish, extravagant, plentiful or abundant.

Optional Words:

excessive	luxuriant	munificent	opulent
prodigal	profligate	liberal	extreme

PROGRESS *(noun)*

forward or onward movement; an advance or development, especially to a better state.

Optional Words:

gain	growth	motion	breakthrough
development	enrichment	headway	advancement
improvement	augmentation		

P

PROJECT *(verb)*

to extend outward from a surface.

Optional Words:

protrude	jut	launch	overhang
overlap	propel		

(verb)

to devise or design.

Optional Words:

visualize	propose	plan	predetermine
scheme	forecast	calculate	

PROJECTION *(noun)*

an estimate of future situations or trends based on a study
of present ones.

Optional Words:

forecast	guess	prediction	approximation
prognostication			

PROMINENT *(adjective)*

important or well-known.

Optional Words:

celebrated	famous	outstanding	prestigious
pronounced	renowned	illustrious	famed
great	notable	eminent	distinguished
leading			

P

PROMISE *(noun)*

a declaration that one will give or do a certain thing.

Optional Words:

assurance	guarantee	vow	commitment
oath	pledge	covenant	contract

PROMOTE *(verb)*

to raise awareness or image; to advertise or publicize.

Optional Words:

advance	boost	champion	elevate
foster	further	upgrade	announce
import	proclaim	plug	

PROMPT *(adjective)*

made, done or doing something without delay.

Optional Words:

immediate	instant	precise	punctual
quick	timely	early	ready
hasty			

PROPEL *(verb)*

to drive or push forward; to give onward movement to.

Optional Words:

catapult	discharge	eject	force
launch	move	project	shoot
start	press		

P

PROPER *(adjective)*

suitable, appropriate or correct; according to rules.

Optional Words:

accurate	appropriate	apropos	exact
fitting	polite	precise	prim
seemly	tasteful		

PROPERTY *(noun)*

a thing or things owned.

Optional Words:

asset	belonging	effect	holding
investment	possession		

(noun)

a quality or characteristic.

Optional Words:

aspect	attribute	trait

PROPHECY *(noun)*

the power of prophesying; a statement that tells what will happen.

Optional Words:

divination	forecast	prediction	revelation
augury	projection	soothsaying	

PROPITIATE *(verb)*

to win favor; to give a good omen or suitable opportunity.

Optional Words:

alleviate	assuage	conciliate	accommodate
mollify	pacify	soothe	satisfy

P

PROPONENT *(noun)*

the person who puts forward a theory or proposal.

Optional Words:

expander	supporter	advocate	champion
exponent	defender		

PROPOSE *(verb)*

to put forward for consideration; to have and declare as one's plan or intention.

Optional Words:

advance	aim	broach	contemplate
plan	pose	project	submit
suggest	offer	contend	assert
submit			

PROPRIETARY *(adjective)*

of an owner or ownership.

Optional Words:

possessive   mastery

PROPRIETY *(noun)*

being proper or suitable; correctness of behavior or morals.

Optional Words:

aptness	suitability	accordance	agreeability
seemliness	congruity	dignity	appropriateness

P

PROSPER *(verb)*

to be successful or thrive.

Optional Words:

flourish	flower	progress	succeed
bloom	score	blossom	benefit
advance			

PROTECT *(verb)*

to keep from harm or injury.

Optional Words:

conserve	cover	defend	guard
maintain	preserve	safeguard	shelter
shield	sustain	buffer	bumper
champion			

PROTOCOL *(noun)*

etiquette with regard to people's rank or status.

Optional Words:

amenities	convention	customs	decorum
propriety			

PROUD *(adjective)*

feeling or showing justifiable pride; full of self-respect and independence.

Optional Words:

delighted	dignified	exalted	distinguished
glorious	honorable	illustrious	magnificent
splendid	stately	sublime	

P

....

PROVE *(verb)*

to give or be proof of; to establish the validity of.

Optional Words:

ascertain	certify	confirm	demonstrate
determine	document	establish	examine
test	verify		

PROVIDE *(verb)*

to cause to have possession or use of something; to supply.

Optional Words:

afford	contribute	dispense	equip
furnish	give	grant	keep
outfit	produce	yield	

PROVIDENT *(adjective)*

showing wise forethought for future needs or events.

Optional Words:

circumspect	discerning	farsighted	thoughtful
cautious	prepared	prudent	judicious
providential			

PRUDENT *(adjective)*

showing carefulness and foresight.

Optional Words:

careful	cautious	discerning	circumspect
discreet	economical	expedient	frugal
judicious	thrifty	parsimonious	

● ● ● ● ● ● ● ● ● ● ● ● ● ● ● ● ● ●

P

PUBLICITY *(noun)*

public attention directed upon a person or thing.

Optional Words:
advertising   coverage   press   promotion
public notice

PUBLISH *(verb)*

to make generally known; to announce formally.

Optional Words:

advertise	distribute	issue	market
print	proclaim	produce	blaze
toot	declare	promulgate	

PULL *(noun)*

a means of exerting influence.

Optional Words:

allure	appeal	attraction	influence
inducement	weight	inclination	

PURCHASE *(verb)*

to buy.

Optional Words:

acquire	obtain	procure	secure
get	shop	invest	

P

PURE *(adjective)*

a singular substance; free from impurities.

Optional Words:

absolute	chaste	genuine	immaculate
perfect	plain	sheer	straight
theoretical	virginal	virtuous	

PURPOSE *(noun)*

an intended result; something for which effort is being made.

Optional Words:

aim	design	function	intention
mission	objective	plan	rationale
reason	resolve		

PURSUANCE *(noun)*

performance or carrying out of something.

Optional Words:

attempt	endeavor	hunt

Q

Section Index

Q

Q

QUAINT *(adjective)*

odd in a pleasing way; attractive through being unusual or old-fashioned.

Optional Words:

bizarre	capricious	charming	curious
fanciful	outlandish	picturesque	unique
whimsical	baroque	cute	enchanting
antique	captivating		

QUALIFY *(verb)*

to make or become competent, eligible or legally entitled to do something.

Optional Words:

authorize   entitle   pass

QUALITY *(noun)*

a degree or level of excellence.

Optional Words:

caliber	merit	value	worth
endowment	class	standing	rank
position			

(noun)

a characteristic; something that is special in a person or thing.

Optional Words:

attribute	distinction	feature	trait
endowment	class		

Q

QUANTITY *(noun)*

a specified number, amount or weight.

Optional Words:

amount	number	bulk	mass
measure	extent	volume	capacity
lot	deal	pile	sum
magnitude	portion	supply	bunch
heap	batch		

QUEEN *(noun)*

a woman, place or thing regarded as supreme in some way.

Optional Words:

ruler	female	sovereign	woman monarch
consort	regent	czarina	queen mother
matriarch			

QUEST *(noun)*

the act of seeking something; a search.

Optional Words:

crusade	endeavor	enterprise	pilgrimage
pursuit	undertaking	venture	journey
hunt			

Q

QUICK *(adjective)*

taking only a short time to do something; able to notice, learn or think quickly; stimulating.

Optional Words:

alert	astute	bright	expeditious
brisk	fast	fleet	immediate
hasty	keen	prompt	instantaneous
rapid	swift	vigorous	posthaste
ready	sharp	lively	

QUINTESSENCE *(noun)*

a perfect example of a quality.

Optional Words:

embodiment	epitome	essence	heart
prototype	substance	spirit	soul
virtuality			

QUOTE *(verb)*

to repeat or write out words from a book or speech; to mention in support of a statement.

Optional Words:

cite	paraphrase	recite	refer to
repeat	excerpt	extract	

R

R

R

RADIATE *(verb)*

to give forth a feeling of.

Optional Words:

emit	give off	transmit	broadcast
propagate	circulate		

(verb)

to give out rays of light; to look very bright and happy.

Optional Words:

beam	emit	gleam	illuminate
shine	irradiate		

RAISE *(verb)*

to bring to or towards a higher or upright position; to heighten the level of.

Optional Words:

boost	build	construct	elevate
erect	foster	hoist	inflate
lift	nurture	produce	rouse
spark	stimulate	exalt	

(verb)

to increase the amount of.

Optional Words:

increase	procure	solicit	collect
amass			

RALLY *(verb)*

to bring or come together for a united effort; to rouse or revive.

Optional Words:

assemble	convene	encourage	gather
hearten	inspire	unite	invigorate
enliven	stir	kindle	challenge
organize	muster	marshal	mobilize

R

....

RANK *(noun)*

a place in a scale of quality or value.

Optional Words:

degree	level	place	classification
order	position	sort	station
status	sphere	caste	state
situation	standing		

(noun)

high social position.

Optional Words:

class	seniority	status	authority
caste	reputation	notability	esteem
standing			

RAPPORT *(noun)*

a harmonious and understanding relationship between people.

Optional Words:

affinity	camaraderie	harmony	compatibility
agreement	concord	unity	understanding

RAPT *(adjective)*

very intent and absorbed; enraptured.

Optional Words:

attentive	captivated	enchanted	overwhelmed
enthralled	spellbound	charmed	transported
beguiled	taken	engrossed	

R

RAPTURE *(noun)*

intense delight or ecstatic joy.

Optional Words:

bliss	elation	euphoria	enchantment
pleasure	thrill	enthusiasm	glory
enjoyment	happiness	gladness	cheer
gratification	satisfaction	jubilation	gaiety
passion	ecstasy		

RARE *(adjective)*

seldom found or occurring; very uncommon.

Optional Words:

exceptional	infrequent	preeminent	extraordinary
remarkable	scarce	singular	unique
unusual	select	superlative	choice
exquisite	superior		

RARING *(adjective)*

enthusiastic (as in raring to go); anxious to get started.

Optional Words:

ambitious	eager	keen	anxious
ardent	avid	thirsty	

RATIFY *(verb)*

to confirm or assent formally and make valid.

Optional Words:

approve	confirm	corroborate	enact
endorse	legalize	legislate	pass
support	sanction	establish	substantiate

R

RATING *(noun)*

the classification assigned to a person or thing in respect of quality or popularity.

Optional Words:

degree	levy	measure	assessment
percentage	proportion		

RATIONAL *(adjective)*

able to reason; based on reasoning; using reason or logic.

Optional Words:

analytic	balanced	cognitive	clearheaded
logical	lucid	reasonable	sane
sensible	sound	wise	stable
discerning	thoughtful	prudent	intellectual

RAVE *(verb)*

to speak with rapturous admiration.

Optional Words:

cheer	effervesce	gush	enthuse
rhapsodize			

RAVISH *(verb)*

to fill with delight; to enrapture.

Optional Words:

delight	overcome	transport	magnetize
fascinate	charm	attract	allure
enthrall	hold		

R

REACH *(verb)*

to stretch out or extend; to go as far as; to arrive at.

Optional Words:

accomplish	achieve	attain	contact
extend	realize	stretch	touch
span	encompass		

REACTION *(noun)*

a response to a stimulus, act or situation.

Optional Words:

answer	effect	reply	response
result	rejoinder	reception	return
feeling	opinion	reflection	attitude
reflex			

READY *(adjective)*

in a fit state for immediate action or use; willing, quick or easily available.

Optional Words:

alert	attentive	swift	eager
equipped	fit	handy	inclined
prepared	primed	present	set
available	at hand	anticipating	waiting
on call	sharp	fast	fleet

R

REAL *(adjective)*

existing as a thing or occurring as a fact; not imaginary or imitation; genuine and true; natural; resembling the original.

Optional Words:

actual	authentic	concrete	factual
genuine	honest	sincere	solid
substantial	substantive	tangible	true
firm	sound	existing	stable
present	in existence	palpable	

REAP *(verb)*

to cut as a harvest; to receive as the consequence of actions.

Optional Words:

acquire	gather	get	glean
harvest	receive	derive	procure
secure	collect	take in	realize
profit	draw		

REASSURE *(verb)*

to give confidence to.

Optional Words:

assure	cheer	encourage	hearten
inspire	convince	console	guarantee

RECEIVE *(verb)*

to acquire, accept or take in; to experience.

Optional Words:

obtain	welcome	procure	appropriate
win	secure	get	gain
inherit	collect	gather up	admit
reap	derive		

RECEPTIVE *(adjective)*

able, quick or willing to receive knowledge, ideas or suggestions.

Optional Words:

alert	astute	bright	flexible
intelligent	interested	perceptive	open-minded
pliant	sympathetic	acceptant	sensitive
observant	persuadable	swayable	influenceable

RECIPROCATE *(verb)*

to give and receive; to make a return for something done, given or felt.

Optional Words:

respond	return	exchange	recompense
requite	repay	interchange	

RECOGNIZE *(verb)*

to acknowledge or accept formally as genuine or valid; to show appreciation of by giving an honor or reward.

Optional Words:

admit	appreciate	place	acknowledge
credit	identify	know	comprehend
realize	understand	assent	distinguish
pinpoint	note		

R

RECOMMEND *(verb)*

to advise; to praise as worthy of employment, favor or trial.

Optional Words:

advocate	approve	compliment	encourage
endorse	extol	praise	promote
suggest	urge	commend	applaud
confirm	laud	second	favor
back	esteem	acclaim	vouch for
value	confirm	uphold	

RECORD *(noun)*

the best performance or most remarkable event of its kind (as in hold the record); the one who achieved this or most extreme.

Optional Words:

victory	feat	triumph	achievement
success	conquest	attainment	performance
masterwork			

RECTITUDE *(noun)*

moral goodness; correctness of behavior or procedure.

Optional Words:

virtue	justness	integrity	scrupulousness
honesty			

RECREATION *(noun)*

the process or means of refreshing or entertaining oneself by some pleasurable activity.

Optional Words:

play	diversion	leisure	entertainment
relaxation	enjoyment	festivity	refreshment
hobby	holiday	pastime	amusement
fun	pleasure		

R

RECUR *(verb)*

to happen again; to keep occurring.

Optional Words:

continue	persist	repeat	resume
return	recrudesce	revert	crop up again
reiterate			

REDEEM *(verb)*

to recover by doing something; to obtain the freedom of by payment.

Optional Words:

cash in	fulfill	keep	rescue
save	buy off	get back	make good
repay	restore	settle	reinstate
acquire			

REFER *(verb)*

to send on or direct (a person) to some authority, specialist or source of information; to mention or allude to.

Optional Words:

cite	direct	mention	point
quote	refer to	advert	ascribe
attribute	hint at	notice	indicate
suggest	touch on	excerpt	speak about
transfer			

REFINE *(verb)*

to make elegant or cultured.

Optional Words:

better	cultivate	develop	improve
perfect	process	purify	enlighten
civilize			

R

REFORM *(verb)*

to make or become better.

Optional Words:

amend	better	change	correct
improve	organize	revise	

REFRESH *(verb)*

to restore the strength and vigor of (a person, etc.) by food, drink or rest.

Optional Words:

invigorate	rejuvenate	renew	animate
exhilarate	refurbish	bring around	

REFULGENT *(adjective)*

shining, gloriously bright.

Optional Words:

brilliant	dazzling	gleaming	glittering
radiant	sparkling	effulgent	resplendent
lambent	lucent	luminous	incandescent

REFURBISH *(verb)*

to make clean or bright again.

Optional Words:

fix up	overhaul	remodel	renovate
restore	update	rejuvenate	renew
repair	refresh	modernize	

REGAL *(adjective)*

like or fit for a king.

Optional Words:

aristocratic	dignified	majestic	noble
royal	stately	sovereign	monarchical
august	kinglike	glorious	imposing

REGALE *(verb)*

to feed or entertain well; to satisfy.

Optional Words:

amuse	delight	dine	entertain
feast	please	nurture	gratify
celebrate			

REGALIA *(plural noun)*

the emblems of royalty used at coronations; the emblems or costumes of an order.

Optional Words:

insignia	decorations	crown	emblem
symbol			

REGARD *(verb)*

to look steadily; to consider to be.

Optional Words:

admire	consider	contemplate	esteem
honor	judge	notice	observe
rate	revere	think	view
surmise	watch	heed	gaze
mark	note	value	appreciate

R

venerate   heed

(noun)
respect.
Optional Words:
concern	esteem	honor	consideration
admiration	homage	appreciation	

REINFORCE *(verb)*

to strengthen or support by additional persons, material or an added quantity.

Optional Words:
augment	bolster	fortify	strengthen
support	buttress	pillar	add to
assist			

REJOICE *(verb)*

to feel or show great joy; to make glad.

Optional Words:
celebrate	exult	glory	revel
triumph	enjoy		

REJUVENATE *(verb)*

to restore youthful appearance or vigor to.

Optional Words:
invigorate	renew	restore	revitalize
revive	rehabilitate	update	renovate
exhilarate	refresh	strengthen	stimulate
modernize			

R

∙ ∙

RELAX *(verb)*

to become or cause to become less tight or tense.

Optional Words:

calm	ease	loosen	repose
rest	slacken	soothe	recline
settle back	take five	unwind	loaf

RELISH *(noun)*

great enjoyment of food or other things.

Optional Words:

enthusiasm	gusto	zest	joy
satisfaction	heart		

(verb)

to enjoy greatly.

Optional Words:

enjoy	like	love	savor

RELY *(verb)*

to trust confidently; to depend on for help, quality, performance, etc.

Optional Words:

bank on	count on	hang	hinge
trust	swear by	build on	expect
hope	put faith in		

R

· ·

REMARKABLE *(adjective)*

worth noticing; exceptional or unusual.

Optional Words:

exceptional	fabulous	incredible	magnificent
outstanding	noticeable	prominent	extraordinary
arresting	salient	conspicuous	striking
marked	important	rare	singular
significant			

REMUNERATIVE *(adjective)*

profitable.

Optional Words:

rewarding	gainful	compensating

RENASCENT *(adjective)*

springing up anew; being reborn.

Optional Words:

reviving

RENDER *(verb)*

to give, especially in return, exchange or as something due.

Optional Words:

give	execute	present	yield
relinquish	supply	surrender	

(verb)
to represent, especially in a drawing or painting.

Optional Words:

delineate	depict	interpret

R

RENEW *(verb)*

to restore to its original state; to replace with a fresh supply.

Optional Words:

maintain	recondition	refurbish	rejuvenate
renovate	restore	revitalize	modernize
update			

RENOWNED *(adjective)*

famous or celebrated.

Optional Words:

acclaimed	notable	popular	distinguished
prominent			

REORGANIZE *(verb)*

to organize in a new way.

Optional Words:

rearrange	reconstitute	reconstruct	reorder
reorient	reestablish	renovate	rebuild

REQUIRE *(verb)*

to need; to depend on for success or fulfillment.

Optional Words:

want	necessitate	crave

R

RESILIENT *(adjective)*

springing back to original form.

Optional Words:

elastic	flexible	hardy	rubbery
springy	stretchy	tenacious	expansive
rebounding	bouncy	buoyant	effervescent

RESOLVE *(verb)*

to decide firmly.

Optional Words:

conclude	determine	settle	rule
choose	elect		

RESOURCE *(noun)*

something to which one can turn for help, support or to achieve one's purpose.

Optional Words:

recourse	refuge	reserve	supply
source	stock	means	stratagem
relief	device	assets	capital
wealth			

RESPECT *(noun)*

admiration felt towards a person or thing that has good qualities or achievements; politeness arising from this; attention and consideration; good social standing.

Optional Words:

admiration	deference	esteem	consideration
honor	regard	reverence	veneration
account	admiration	estimation	favor
awe	adoration		

RESPONSIBILITY (noun)

the state or quality of being responsible.

Optional Words:

loyalty	faithfulness	ability	steadfastness
liability	efficiency	competency	dependability
stability			

(noun)

that for which one is answerable; a duty.

Optional Words:

pledge	contract	burden	obligation

RESULT *(noun)*

that which is produced by an activity or operation; an effect.

Optional Words:

conclusion	corollary	fallout	consequence
outcome	event	execution	consummation
aftermath	proceeds	eventuality	outgrowth

RESUME *(verb)*

to get, take or occupy again; to begin again.

Optional Words:

continue	proceed	recommence	restart
go on (with)	reoccupy	return	

RETAIN *(verb)*

to keep in one's possession; to continue to have.

Optional Words:

care for	conserve	endure	hold
hinder	keep from	maintain	persist
preserve	prevent	reserve	

R

. . . .

RETURN *(verb)*

to come or go back; to bring, give, put or send back.

Optional Words:

come back	refund	reinstate	repay
replace	yield	reappear	rebound
recover	reoccur	revisit	repeat

REUNITE *(verb)*

to unite again.

Optional Words:

reassemble	reconvene	rejoin	reconcile

REVAMP *(verb)*

to renovate; to give a new appearance to.

Optional Words:

overhaul	redo	remodel	rejuvenate
replenish	fix	recondition	reconstruct
renew	repair	mend	

REVEAL *(verb)*

to make known; to uncover and allow to be seen.

Optional Words:

announce	divulge	impart	communicate
proclaim	relate	show	declare
broadcast	publish	disclose	inform

REVEL *(verb)*

to take great delight; to enjoy.

Optional Words:

bask	celebrate	delight	enjoy
frolic	rejoice	relish	

(noun)

lively festivities or merrymaking.

Optional Words:

celebration	fling	spree	fete
festival	party		

REVELATION *(noun)*

something revealed, especially something surprising.

Optional Words:

discovery	divulgement disclosure	announcement

REVERE *(verb)*

to feel deep respect.

Optional Words:

admire	worship	defer	venerate
awe	devote	adore	honor
regard	respect	cherish	prize
treasure	exalt	esteem	appreciate

R

REVIVE *(verb)*

to come or bring back to life, consciousness or strength.

Optional Words:

activate	animate	awaken	rekindle
renew	revitalize	restore	repair
rejuvenate	recondition	enliven	enkindle
resurrect	refresh	vivify	exhilarate
energize			

REVOLVE *(verb)*

to turn or cause to turn; to rotate.

Optional Words:

gyrate	spin	whirl	twirl
circle	circumvent		

REWARD *(noun)*

something given or received in return for a service or merit.

Optional Words:

award	bonus	grant	compensation
honorarium	payment	prize	remuneration
pay	premium	dividend	

RHAPSODIZE *(verb)*

to talk or write about something in an ecstatic way.

Optional Words:

enthuse	rave	extol	acclaim
praise	glorify	exalt	

R

RHETORIC *(noun)*

the art of using words impressively; language used for its impressive sound; affected or exaggerated expressions.

Optional Words:

discourse	elocution	oratory	rodomontade
utterance	verbosity	bombast	lexicography

RICH *(adjective)*

having much wealth; having a large supply of something such as property or valuable possessions.

Optional Words:

abundant	affluent	fertile	fruitful
prosperous	wealthy	comfortable	well-off
moneyed	bounteous	well-to-do	

(adjective)
magnificent.

Optional Words:

lavish	lush	luxurious	opulent
splendid	sumptuous	auspicious	flourishing

RIGHT *(adjective)*

morally good; in accordance with justice; proper, correct or true; morally justified.

Optional Words:

accurate	actual	authentic	directly
ethical	exact	exactly	fitting
genuine	honest	just	moral
precise	real	upright	valid
seemly	suitable	appropriate	

R

RISE *(verb)*

to come or go upwards; to grow or extend upwards; to achieve a higher position or status.

Optional Words:

ascend	build	climb	escalate
get up	intensify	mount	multiply
soar	stand		

ROBUST *(adjective)*

strong and vigorous.

Optional Words:

athletic	energetic	flavorful	hardy
hefty	husky	lively	loud
rich	rugged	solid	substantial

ROLLICKING *(adjective)*

full of boisterous high spirits.

Optional Words:

fun	gleeful	happy	jolly
lively	merry	playful	jovial
sportive	jaunty		

ROMANTIC *(adjective)*

appealing to the emotions by imaginative, heroic or picturesque quality.

Optional Words:

amorous	ardent	fanciful	fictitious
illusory	imaginary	loving	passionate
sensitive	sentimental	tender	

R

ROMP *(verb)*

to play in a lively way, as children do.

Optional Words:

celebrate	frolic	revel	rollick
gambol	caper	frisk	skip
cavort	spring		

ROUSE *(verb)*

to cause to become active or excited.

Optional Words:

induce	prompt	stimulate	inspirit
animate	incite	provoke	instigate

ROYAL *(adjective)*

suitable for or worthy of a king or queen; splendid or first-rate; of exceptional size.

Optional Words:

imperial	kingly	majestic	noble
princely	queenly	regal	greathearted
stately	elevated	monarchic	resplendent
august	lordly	superb	sublime

RULER *(noun)*

a person who rules by authority.

Optional Words:

chief	commander	dictator	emperor
leader	monarch	president	potentate
director	sovereign	governor	adjudicator
regent			

R

●●●●●●●●●●●●●●●●●●●●●●●●●●●

RULING *(noun)*

an authoritative decision.

Optional Words:
decree   judgment   order   pronouncement
precept

RUN *(verb)*

to move with quick steps; to never have both or all feet on
the ground at once.

Optional Words:
bolt   dart   dash   sprint

(verb)
to compete in a race or contest.

Optional Words:
compete   race

(verb)
to seek election.

Optional Words:
campaign

(verb)
to flow or cause to flow; to function; to be in action.

Optional Words:
control   drive   operate   propel
spread   stream

RUSH *(verb)*

to go, come or convey with great speed.

Optional Words:

accelerate	advance	charge	dash
expedite	gush	hasten	hurry
race	sally	surge	

(noun)

a period of great activity.

Optional Words:

blitz	charge

S

SAFE
SAGE
SAINTLY
SALE
SALUTATION
SANCTION
SANCTITY
SAPIENT
SATISFY
SAVE
SAVVY
SCENT
SCHEME
SCHOLAR
SCOPE
SCRUPULOUS
SECURITY
SEEMLY
SELECT
SELF-ASSERTIVE
SELF-COMMAND
SELF-CONFIDENT
SELF-DETERMINA-
TION
SELL
SEND
SENSATION
SENSE
SENSUOUS
SENTIMENTAL
SERENDIPITY
SERENE
SERVE
SERVICEABLE
SET

SETTLE
SEVERAL
SHARE
SHARP
SHELTER
SHIELD
SHINE
SHOUT
SHOW
SHOWMANSHIP
SIGNAL
SIGNIFICANCE
SILKEN
SIMILAR
SIMPLY
SINCERE
SING
SINGULAR
SLEEK
SLENDER
SMART
SMASHING
SMOOTH
SNAPPY
SOCIAL
SOCIETY
SOFT
SOIREE
SOLEMNIZE
SOLID
SOLIDARITY
SOLVE
SOON
SOOTHE
SOPHISTICATED

SOUND
SOVEREIGN
SPARKLE
SPECIAL
SPECIFIC
SPECTACLE
SPECTRUM
SPEED
SPICE
SPIRIT
SPLENDID
SPONSOR
SPORTSMANLIKE
SPREE
SPRIGHTLY
SPRING
SPRUCE
SPURT
STABLE
STACK
STAGE
STANDARD
STANDPOINT
STAR
START
STATE
STATURE
STAUNCH
STAY
STEADFAST
STEADY
STIMULATE
STIRRING
STRAIGHT
STRATEGY

S

STRENGTH
STRETCH
STRIVE
STROKE
STROLL
STRONG
STUDY
STUPENDOUS
STYLE
SUAVE
SUBMIT
SUBSCRIBE
SUBSTANTIAL
SUCCEED
SUITABLE
SUMPTUOUS
SUNBEAM
SUNSHINE
SUPER
SUPERB
SUPERABUNDANT
SUPEREROGATE
SUPERFINE
SUPERFLUOUS
SUPERHUMAN
SUPERIOR
SUPERLATIVE
SUPPORT
SUPREME
SURE
SURPRISE
SWEET
SWIFT

S

SAFE *(adjective)*

providing security or protection.

Optional Words:

cautious	guarded	protected	circumspect
prudent	secure	sheltered	housed
supported	sustained	watched	

SAGE *(adjective)*

profoundly wise; having wisdom gained from experience.

Optional Words:

learned	sagacious	sapient	wise
expert	master		

SAINTLY *(adjective)*

being of deep religious and wholly upright character; very good, patient or unselfish.

Optional Words:

angelic	holy	godly	devout
pious	righteous	upright	virtuous
worthy	divine		

SALE *(noun)*

selling or being sold; exchange or transfer of property for money.

Optional Words:

bargain	trade	traffic	vending
barter	deal	exchange	commerse
business	marketing		

S

SALUTATION *(noun)*

a word, words or gesture of greeting; an expression of respect or admiration.

Optional Words:

accolade	applause	greeting	honor
recognition	citation	encomium	tribute
address	welcome	regards	

SANCTION *(noun)*

permission or approval for an action or behavior.

Optional Words:

confirmation	consent	license	encouragement
commission	approbation	ratification	countenance

(verb)

to give sanction or approval to; to authorize.

Optional Words:

condone	consent	endorse	support
commission	license	certify	countenance

SANCTITY *(noun)*

sacredness, holiness or solemnity.

Optional Words:

saintliness	godliness	piety	righteousness
			uprighteousness

SAPIENT *(adjective)*

wise.

Optional Words:

discerning	judicious	learned	perspicacious
sagacious	sage	shrewd	prudent
sensible	sane	erudite	discriminating

SATISFY *(verb)*

to give (a person) what he or she wants or needs; to make pleased or contented; to gratify a feeling.

Optional Words:

appease	suffice	fulfill	gratify
mollify	pacify	please	quench
sate	satiate	assure	answer
comply	comfort	cheer	elate
rejoice	provide	furnish	serve
meet	avail		

SAVE *(verb)*

to rescue.

Optional Words:

conserve	free	protect	recover
redeem	safeguard	salvage	extricate
preserve			

(verb)
to put aside, as a reserve.

Optional Words:

economize	reserve	retrench	withhold

(verb)
to keep.

Optional Words:

conserve	preserve	store	withhold

SAVVY *(noun slang)*

common sense and understanding.

Optional Words:

good sense	sagacious	astute	comprehension
perspicacious			

S

SCENT *(noun)*

the characteristic pleasant smell of something; a sweet-smelling liquid made from essence of flowers or aromatic chemicals.

Optional Words:

aroma	bouquet	cologne	fragrance
perfume	smell	redolence	

SCHEME *(noun)*

a plan of work or action; an orderly, planned arrangement.

Optional Words:

chart	design	diagram	layout
method	outline	plan	plot
procedure	strategy		

SCHOLAR *(noun)*

a person with great learning in a particular subject.

Optional Words:

intellectual	professor	teacher	sage
savant	wise man	expert	academic
doctor	litterateur	master	

SCOPE *(noun)*

the range of something; capacity for achievement or effectiveness; opportunity; outlet.

Optional Words:

breadth	radius	extent	range
reach	leeway	margin	latitude
orbit			

SCRUPULOUS *(adjective)*

very conscientious, even in small matters; painstakingly careful and thorough; strictly honest or honorable.

Optional Words:

careful	ethical	exact	conscientious
honest	meticulous	precise	principled
upright	just	upstanding	fastidious
punctilious	strict		

SECURITY *(noun)*

a state or feeling of being secure; something that gives this.

Optional Words:

assurance	certainty	confidence	protection
safety	strength	sureness	stability

(noun)

a thing that serves as a guarantee or pledge.

Optional Words:

bond	certificate	collateral	deposit
guarantee	stock		

SEEMLY *(adjective)*

proper or suitable; in accordance with accepted standards of good taste.

Optional Words:

appropriate	attractive	comely	decorous
handsome	pretty	decent	becoming
fitting	correct	right	

S

SELECT *(adjective)*

chosen for excellence; singled out from a group by fitness or preference.

Optional Words:

choice	elect	elite	prime
superior	exclusive	culled	screened
favored	best	eclectic	

SELF-ASSERTIVE *(adjective)*

asserting oneself confidently.

Optional Words:

forward	sure	assertive	swaggering
impudent			

SELF-COMMAND *(noun)*

self-control; the state of having one's faculties and powers fully and effectively at command.

Optional Words:

will	discipline	willpower	self-mastery

SELF-CONFIDENT *(adjective)*

having confidence in one's own abilities.

Optional Words:
self-assured self-trusting sureness

SELF-DETERMINATION *(noun)*

determination of one's own fate or course of action.

Optional Words:
free will   **self-decision**   **self-decidedness**

SELL *(verb)*

to transfer the ownership of (goods, etc.) in exchange for money; to persuade a person into accepting (a thing) by convincing him or her of its merits.

Optional Words:

handle	hawk	market	merchandise
peddle	retail	vend	barter
exchange	trade		

SEND *(verb)*

to order, cause or enable to go to a certain destination.

Optional Words:

direct	dispatch	guide	issue
mail	refer	relay	route
ship			

(verb)
to have (a thing) conveyed.

Optional Words:
broadcast   **transmit**   **address**

S

SENSATION *(noun)*

an awareness or feeling.

Optional Words:
feeling	impression	intuition	presentiment
perception	sense		

(noun)

a condition of eager interest, excitement or admiration.

Optional Words:
commotion	excitement	stir	phenomenon
wonder	marvel	portent	

SENSE *(noun)*

any of the special powers by which a living thing becomes aware of things; ability to perceive, feel or be conscious of a thing.

Optional Words:
connotation	faculty	feeling	understanding
judgment	logic	meaning	perception
reason	sensation	purport	significance
function			

SENSUOUS *(adjective)*

affecting or appealing to the senses, especially by beauty or delicacy.

Optional Words:
appealing	delicious	delightful	exquisite
luscious	sensory	sumptuous	epicurean
luxurious	lush	sensual	

SENTIMENTAL *(adjective)*

showing or influenced by romantic or nostalgic feeling; characterized by emotions as opposed to reason.

Optional Words:

emotional   nostalgic   romantic   melodramatic
effusive   dreamy

SERENDIPITY *(noun)*

the making of pleasant discoveries by accident; the knack of doing this.

Optional Words:

chance   coincidence   fortuity   fortune
luck   providence   canniness

SERENE *(adjective)*

calm and cheerful.

Optional Words:

collected   composed   halcyon   even-tempered
peaceful   placid   tranquil   self-controlled
poised   quiet   still   easygoing

SERVE *(verb)*

to perform services for.

Optional Words:

aid   assist   attend   benefit
better   care for   facilitate   function
further   help   minister to   oblige
perform   wait on

S

SERVICEABLE (adjective)

suitable for ordinary use or wear.

Optional Words:

durable	functional	lasting	operative
sturdy	tough	usable	useful

SET (verb)

to put or place; to cause to stand in position; to fix, decide or appoint.

Optional Words:

adjust	arrange	assign	congeal
determine	establish	gel	lay
order	position	solidify	station

SETTLE (verb)

to place so that something stays in position.

Optional Words:

alight	conclude	confirm	decide
determine	establish	inhabit	judge
land	locate	mediate	perch
rectify	resolve	situate	

(verb)
to make or become calm or orderly.

Optional Words:

calm	pacify	soothe

SEVERAL (adjective)

a few; more than two.

Optional Words:

many	numerous	some

SHARE *(verb)*

to give away part of.

Optional Words:

allocate	allot	divide	mete out
part	proportion	prorate	ration

SHARP *(adjective)*

quick to see or hear or notice things; intelligent.

Optional Words:

acute	bright	clever	discerning
honed	intelligent	keen	penetrating
perceptive	rapid	alert	brilliant
knowing	clear	distinct	quick-witted

(adjective)
having a cutting edge.

Optional Words:

edged	piercing	pointed	spiked

SHELTER *(noun)*

something that serves as a place of safety or refuge; a shielded condition.

Optional Words:

haven	housing	lodging	protection
quarters	sanctuary		

S

SHIELD *(noun)*

an object, structure or layer of material that protects something.

Optional Words:

aegis	armor	buckler	buffer
cover	guard	protection	security
safeguard			

SHINE *(verb)*

to give out or reflect light; to be bright or glow.

Optional Words:

beam	gleam·	glisten	glitter
glow	radiate	scintillate	sparkle
sheen	glimmer	luminesce	

(verb)

to excel in some way.

Optional Words:

exceed	transcend	surpass	eclipse
prevail			

(verb)

to polish.

Optional Words:

polish	smooth	burnish

SHOUT *(noun)*

a loud cry or utterance of words calling attention or expressing joy, excitement or disapproval.

Optional Words:

cheer	cry	howl	hurrah
roar	whoop	bellow	call
yell			

SHOW *(verb)*

to demonstrate; to point out; to prove; to cause to understand; to present an image of.

Optional Words:

bare	confirm	exhibit	demonstrate
explain	expose	mark	pose
reveal	disclose	establish	

(noun)

a public exhibition for competition, entertainment or advertisement.

Optional Words:

affectation	display	drama	demonstration
exhibit	pose	spectacle	manifestation
pretense	production	program	presentation

SHOWMANSHIP *(noun)*

skill in presenting an entertainment, goods or one's abilities to the best advantage; displaying brilliance.

Optional Words:

talent	ingenuity	genius	dramatization

SIGNAL *(noun)*

a sign or gesture giving information or a command; a message made up of such signs.

Optional Words:

alarm	beacon	bell	blinker
buzzer	flag	flare	indication
siren	warning		

S

SIGNIFICANCE *(noun)*

what is meant by something; importance.

Optional Words:

aim	implication	intention	consequence
meaning	object	purpose	relevance
weight			

SILKEN *(adjective)*

like silk; glossy, delicate, smooth and luxurious.

Optional Words:

soft	velvety	tender

SIMILAR *(adjective)*

of the same kind, nature or amount.

Optional Words:

alike	analogous	coinciding	corresponding
like	parallel	related	comparable

SIMPLY *(adverb)*

absolutely; without doubt; easy to do or understand.

Optional Words:

clearly	directly	intelligibly	merely
only	plainly	easily	naturally
frankly			

• •

SINCERE *(adjective)*

honest in feeling, manner or actions.

Optional Words:

candid	faithful	frank	genuine
ingenuous	straight	forward	true
heartfelt	plain	forthright	aboveboard
devout	bonafied	truthful	trustworthy

SING *(verb)*

to make musical sounds with the voice.

Optional Words:

carol	chant	croon	intone
serenade	vocalize	tune	troll
cantillate	chirp		

SINGULAR *(adjective)*

extraordinary or remarkable; uncommon or unique.

Optional Words:

outlandish	special	individual	noteworthy
peculiar	exclusive	distinctive	exceptional
eccentric			

SLEEK *(adjective)*

smooth and glossy; looking well-fed and thriving.

Optional Words:

elegant	lustrous	polished	well-groomed
slick	suave		

• • • • • • • • • • • •

S

SLENDER *(adjective)*

slim and graceful.

Optional Words:

lean	slight	thin	willowy
small	svelte	twiggy	spare
tenuous	reedy	skinny	stalky

SMART *(adjective)*

clever or ingenious.

Optional Words:

bright	bold	intelligent	resourceful
witty	wise	canny	knowing
quick	brilliant	hip	

(adjective)

neat and elegant.

Optional Words:

chic	stylish	fashionable

SMASHING *(adjective)*

excellent; extremely impressive or overwhelmingly good.

Optional Words:

dashing	grand	splendid	fashionable
sumptuous	gorgeous		

S

∙ ∙

SMOOTH *(adjective)*

having an even surface with no projections; even in sound or taste.

Optional Words:

constant	debonair	flat	graceful
level	mild	peaceful	regular
steady	suave	uniform	polish
perfect	steady		

(verb)

to create peace and calm.

Optional Words:

flatten	iron	level	polish
steady	perfect		

SNAPPY *(adjective)*

brisk and vigorous; neat and elegant; stylish in appearance.

Optional Words:

vivacious	energetic	smart	dashing
pert	cute	zesty	spicy
racy	piquant		

SOCIAL *(adjective)*

of or designed for companionship and sociability.

Optional Words:

friendly	gregarious	neighborly	pleasant
sociable	gracious	genial	entertaining
cordial	convivial		

S

· ·

SOCIETY *(noun)*

an organized community; a group of people organized for some common purpose.

Optional Words:

association	circle	club	community
league	order	populace	organization

(noun)

people of the higher social classes.

Optional Words:

aristocracy	elite	nobility	gentry

SOFT *(adjective)*

gentle, soothing and comfortable.

Optional Words:

delicate	downy	faint	compassionate
flexible	fluffy	kind	muted
pliable	satiny	silky	subdued
supple	tender	velvety	temperate
moderate	lenient	mild	smooth

SOIREE *(noun)*

a social gathering in the evening; a reception held at night.

Optional Words:

event	party

SOLEMNIZE *(verb)*

to celebrate; to perform with formal rites; to dignify with a ceremony.

Optional Words:

observe	honor	venerate	commemorate
worship			

S

....

SOLID *(adjective)*

sound and reliable; unanimous.

Optional Words:

compact	concrete	continuous	dense
dependable	firm	fixed	hard
material	reliable	rooted	stable
steadfast	steady	substantial	trustworthy

SOLIDARITY *(noun)*

unity resulting from common interests or feelings.

Optional Words:

concord	cooperation	fellowship	togetherness
harmony	unity	cohesion	oneness
union			

SOLVE *(verb)*

to find the answer to.

Optional Words:

elucidate	resolve	settle	work out
fix	determine	decide	explain

SOON *(adverb)*

in a short time; shortly after the present or a specified time; quickly.

Optional Words:

directly	forthwith	presently	expeditiously
fleetingly	hastily	rapidly	posthaste

S

SOOTHE *(verb)*

to have a calming or relieving effect; to smooth or soften.

Optional Words:

allay	becalm	compose	lull
still	settle	tranquilize	hush
subdue	quiet		

SOPHISTICATED *(adjective)*

characteristic of fashionable life and its ways; elaborate.

Optional Words:

advanced	complex	cultured	cosmopolitan
refined	urbane	well-bred	adult
mature			

SOUND *(adjective)*

healthy; correct, logical or well-founded; financially secure; thorough.

Optional Words:

competent	fit	hardy	intact
sensible	solid	stable	sturdy

. . . .

SOVEREIGN *(adjective)*

supreme or very effective.

Optional Words:
lofty	fine	excellent	paramount
dominant	champion		

(adjective)
possessing sovereign power.

Optional Words:
majestic	regal	kingly	ascendant
royal			

(adjective)
independent.

Optional Words:
autonomous

SPARKLE *(verb)*

to shine brightly with flashes of light; to show brilliant wit or liveliness.

Optional Words:
bubble	effervesce	fizz	glisten
glitter	scintillate	shimmer	coruscate
glint	gleam		

SPECIAL *(adjective)*

of a particular kind; for a particular purpose; not general; exceptional in amount, quality or intensity.

Optional Words:
distinct	distinctive	exclusive	exceptional
express	particular	singular	extraordinary
specific	unique	unusual	

SPECIFIC *(adjective)*

particular; clearly distinguished from others; expressing oneself in exact terms; clearly and definitely.

Optional Words:

certain	definite	distinctive	exact
express	individual	precise	unique
explicit	categorical	set	special

SPECTACLE *(noun)*

a striking or impressive sight; a lavish public show or pageant.

Optional Words:

curiosity	display	exhibition	demonstration
marvel	presentation	production	phenomenon
sight	wonder		

SPECTRUM *(noun)*

an entire range of related qualities or ideas.

Optional Words:

sweep	width	reach	realm
scope	panorama	radius	variation
extent			

SPEED *(noun)*

rapidity of movement.

Optional Words:

quickness	swiftness	velocity	acceleration
haste	rush	dispatch	momentum
clip	alacrity	celerity	charge
fastpace	tempo		

SPICE *(noun)*

a thing that adds zest or excitement.

Optional Words:

flavoring	seasoning	zest	zip
dash	tingle		

SPIRIT *(noun)*

a person's nature.

Optional Words:

essence	intent	life	mood
sense	soul	tone	

(noun)
a person with specified mental or moral qualities.

(noun)
liveliness; readiness to assert oneself.

Optional Words:

devotion	loyalty	vigor	animation
vivacity	energy	zest	flamboyance

SPLENDID *(adjective)*

magnificent; displaying splendor; brilliant.

Optional Words:

glorious	gorgeous	grand	marvelous
fine	bright	luxurious	resplendent
sumptuous	superb	exquisite	flamboyant
impressive	lavish	sublime	

S

SPONSOR *(noun)*

a person or firm that provides funds for a broadcast or other special event.

Optional Words:

advocate	backer	champion	patron
supporter	angel	promoter	

SPORTSMANLIKE *(adjective)*

behaving fairly and generously; conforming to the rules of honor.

Optional Words:

fair	equitable	decent	honest
lawful	even	straight	just
candid			

SPREE *(noun)*

a lively outing; some fun.

Optional Words:

fling	splurge	frolic	revel
celebration	festival		

SPRIGHTLY (adjective)

full of animation and spirits; vivacious; lively.

Optional Words:

airy	active	agile	jolly
brisk	cheerful	vivid	joyous
quick	saucy	nimble	spry
happy	gay	jaunty	blithe

S

SPRING *(verb)*

to jump; to move rapidly or suddenly, especially in a single movement.

Optional Words:

bound	hop	leap	emerge
lope	hurdle	vault	bounce

SPRUCE *(adjective)*

neat and trim in appearance; smart.

Optional Words:

fastidious	sassy	spiffy	dapper
slick	natty		

SPURT *(noun)*

a short burst of activity; a sudden increase in speed.

Optional Words:

burst	eruption	flash	outbreak
outburst	rush	surge	

STABLE *(adjective)*

firmly fixed or established.

Optional Words:

balanced	calm	constant	fixed
motionless	placid	secure	sensible
stationary	steady	solid	sturdy
sure			

S

STACK (noun)

an orderly pile or heap; a large quantity.

Optional Words:

collection	mass	hill	accumulation
mound	pyramid	aggregation	

STAGE (verb)

to present; to arrange and carry out; to organize things.

Optional Words:

act	perform	produce	show
put on	execute	play	do
manage	mount		

STANDARD (noun)

a specified level of proficiency.

Optional Words:

archetype	average	criterion	requirement
gauge	ideal	measure	model
pattern	norm	usual	

(adjective)

of recognized merit or authority.

Optional Words:

average	ideal	model	conventional
ordinary	orthodox	regular	usual

STANDPOINT (noun)

a point of view.

Optional Words:

angle	attitude	bias	conviction
opinion	position	slant	stance
view	viewpoint		

• •

STAR *(noun)*

a brilliant person.

Optional Words:
**celebrity   hero   heroine   lead
performer**

START *(verb)*

to begin or cause; to begin a process or course of action;
to establish or found; to spring or rouse.

Optional Words:
**activate   begin   embark   found
inaugurate   initiate   launch   originate
propel   commence   open**

STATE *(noun)*

a condition of being, as in a state of confusion.

Optional Words:
**attitude   condition   mood   circumstance
morale   spirit**

(verb)
to express in spoken or written words.

Optional Words:
assert

• • • • • • • • • • • • •

S

STATURE *(noun)*

the natural height of the body.

Optional Words:

build	height	position	size

(noun)

greatness gained by ability or achievement; high rank or prestige.

Optional Words:

altitude	elevation	eminence	position
rank	standing	quality	prominence
merit	value	virtue	competence
worth			

STAUNCH *(adjective)*

firm in attitude, opinion or loyalty.

Optional Words:

constant	firm	faithful	loyal
stable	stalwart	steadfast	strong
true	zealous	fast	secure
ardent	resolute		

STAY *(verb)*

to continue to be in the same place or state; to remain.

Optional Words:

continue	linger	remain	stop
abide			

(verb)

to satisfy temporarily; to show endurance.

Optional Words:

postpone	tarry

STEADFAST *(adjective)*

firm, not changing or yielding; firmly fixed in faith or devotion to duty.

Optional Words:

constant	faithful	staunch	strong
zealous	adamant	abiding	enduring
allegiant	liege	resolute	wholehearted

STEADY *(adjective)*

firmly supported or balanced.

Optional Words:

even	firm	solid	sturdy

(adjective)

behaving in a dependable manner.

Optional Words:

dedicated	faithful	reliable	conscientious
staunch	steadfast		

(adjective)

free from change or fluctuation.

Optional Words:

consistent	constant	continuous	persistent
habitual	patient	regular	frequent

STIMULATE *(verb)*

to make more vigorous or active; to rouse a person or thing to activity or energy.

Optional Words:

activate	animate	arouse	awaken
encourage	excite	incite	inspire
kindle	prompt	quicken	spur
stir	exhilarate	pique	galvanize
motivate	move		

S

STIRRING *(adjective)*

exciting and stimulating.

Optional Words:

inspiring	busy	dramatic	exhilarating
moving	rousing	thrilling	intoxicating
eye-popping			

STRAIGHT *(adjective)*

correctly arranged; in proper order.

Optional Words:

aligned	continuous	even	linear
neat	nonstop	orderly	pure
square	tidy	plumb	

(adjective)
right or direct.

Optional Words:

candid	direct	forthright	frank
honest	moral	pure	upright
virtuous			

STRATEGY *(noun)*

the planning and directing of an operation; a plan or policy
to achieve something; an advantage.

Optional Words:

approach	artifice	craft	design
system	tactic	project	scheme

STRENGTH *(noun)*

the quality of being strong; the particular respect in which a person or thing is strong.

Optional Words:

brawn	courage	energy	fortitude
grit	might	muscle	vigor
vitality	potency	sturdiness	firmness
soundness	substance	power	force

STRETCH *(verb)*

to pull into a greater length, extent or size.

Optional Words:

cover	elongate	expand	extend
span	traverse	prolong	increase
swell	reach		

STRIVE *(verb)*

to make great efforts.

Optional Words:

attempt	battle	contend	endeavor
labor	try	vie	moil
strain	toil	tug	work

S

STROKE *(noun)*

a single movement, action or effort.

Optional Words:

dash	line	mark	deed
blow			

(noun)

a successful or skillful effort.

Optional Words:

stratagem	coup	victory	conquest

STROLL *(verb)*

to walk in a leisurely way.

Optional Words:

amble	jaunt	ramble	saunter
tour	walk	wander	

STRONG *(adjective)*

having power of resistance to being broken; capable of exerting great power.

Optional Words:

solid	sound	sturdy	reestablished
hard	fixed	anchored	reinforced
rigid	stable	secure	resistant
braced	fortified		

(adjective)
physically powerful.

Optional Words:

brawny	hale	hardy	mighty
muscular	powerful	robust	

(adjective)
powerful through numbers, resources or quality.

Optional Words:

clear	earnest	zealous

(adjective)
concentrated; having a considerable effect on one of the senses.

Optional Words:

ardent	convincing	definite	distinct

STUDY *(noun)*

the process of studying; the pursuit of some branch of knowledge.

Optional Words:

analysis	deliberation	education	contemplation
examination	inquiry	instruction	investigation
probe			

S

STUPENDOUS *(adjective)*

amazing; exceedingly great.

Optional Words:

astounding	colossal	enormous	extraordinary
gigantic	incredible	marvelous	monumentous
massive	tremendous	fantastic	staggering
prodigious	monumental	miraculous	

STYLE *(noun)*

the manner of writing, speaking or doing something.

Optional Words:

manner	method	mode	technique

(noun)
shape or design.

Optional Words:

form

(noun)
elegance.

Optional Words:

charm	class	grace	affluence
luxury	élan	savior-faire	

(noun)
prevailing fashion.

Optional Words:

fad	fashion	trend	vogue

SUAVE *(adjective)*

smooth-mannered.

Optional Words:

cultured	diplomatic	gracious	sophisticated
urbane	agreeable	pleasant	politic

SUBMIT *(verb)*

to present for consideration or decision.

Optional Words:

introduce	propose	suggest	theorize
offer	tender		

SUBSCRIBE *(verb)*

to express one's agreement; to give sanction, support or approval.

Optional Words:

promise	agree	consent	endorse
favor	sanction	acquiesce	contribute

SUBSTANTIAL *(adjective)*

of considerable amount, intensity or validity; possessing much property or wealth.

Optional Words:

abundant	affluent	ample	considerable
important	massive	meaningful	plentiful
prosperous	solid	sound	stable
tangible	thriving	wealthy	

SUCCEED *(verb)*

to be successful; to attain wealth, fame or position.

Optional Words:

accomplish	achieve	flourish	prosper
score	thrive	boom	attain
reach	gain	effect	fulfill
conquer	prevail	win	triumph
beat	finish	overcome	acquire
dominate	reap	outdistance	effectuate

S

················

SUITABLE *(adjective)*

right for the purpose or occasion.

Optional Words:

acceptable	agreeable	appropriate	apropos
congruous	correct	felicitous	fitting
germane	harmonious	pertinent	proper
relevant	seasonable	seemly	timely

SUMPTUOUS *(noun)*

involving or showing lavishness.

Optional Words:

luxurious	opulent	ample	bounteous
copious	plenteous		

SUNBEAM *(noun)*

a beam of sunlight.

Optional Words:

ray	beam	streak

SUNSHINE *(noun)*

direct sunlight; shinning light of the sun.

Optional Words:

light	light of day

(noun)

any cheering influence.

Optional Words:

geniality	gaiety	cheerfulness

SUPER *(prefix)*

over; beyond.

Optional Words:

above	upon	over	more than

(prefix)

superior in number or quality.

Optional Words:

extremely   extra

SUPERABUNDANT *(adjective)*

excessive; more than sufficient.

Optional Words:

exuberant	abounding	plenteous	overflowing
excess	surplus	rampant	epidemic
plentiful			

SUPEREROGATE *(verb)*

to do more than is required or ordered.

Optional Words:

drench	inundate	deluge	flood

SUPERFINE *(adjective)*

of surpassing finesse and delicacy; of the best quality.

Optional Words:

elaborate	intricate	ornate	embellished
elegant	wonderful	fancy	

S

SUPERFLUOUS *(adjective)*

exceeding what is needed; excessively abundant.

Optional Words:

excess   extra   gratuitous   supererogatory
dispensable

SUPERHUMAN *(adjective)*

above the range of human power or skill; miraculous or divine.

Optional Words:

superior   unearthly   uncanny   preternatural
numinous   supernatural

SUPERB *(adjective)*

of the most impressive or splendid kind; excellent.

Optional Words:

admirable   choice   estimable   distinguished
exquisite   magnificent   marvelous   praiseworthy
splendid   sumptuous

SUPERIOR *(adjective)*

higher in position or rank.

(adjective)
better or greater in some way; of high or higher quality.

Optional Words:

inordinate   choice   excellent   exceptional
preferred   immense   huge   first-rate

SUPERLATIVE *(adjective)*

of the highest degree or quality; of supreme excellence or eminence.

Optional Words:

prime	**greatest**	**best**	**excellent**

SUPPORT *(verb)*

to give strength to.

Optional Words:

brace	**prop**

(verb)

to enable to last or continue.

Optional Words:

maintain	**advance**	**finance**	**promote**
fund	**subsidize**	**sustain**	

(verb)

to assist by one's approval or presence.

Optional Words:

advocate	**bolster**	**help**	**champion**
aid			

SUPREME *(adjective)*

highest in authority or rank; highest in importance, intensity or quality.

Optional Words:

absolute	**dominant**	**ideal**	**leading**
matchless	**peerless**	**principal**	**sovereign**
ultimate	**paramount**	**chief**	

S

SURE *(adjective)*

having or seeming to have sufficient reason for one's beliefs; certain to do something or to happen; reliable and secure.

Optional Words:

assured	confident	convinced	definite
dependable	faithful	firm	trustworthy
positive	stable		

SURPRISE *(noun)*

the emotion aroused by something sudden or unexpected; an event or thing that arouses this emotion.

Optional Words:

amazement	wonder	eye-opener	astonishment
incredulity	revelation	shock	astound
flabbergast			

SWEET *(adjective)*

tasting as if containing sugar; fragrant; melodious fresh; pleasant, gratifying, charming or having a pleasant nature.

Optional Words:

agreeable	clean	dulcet	fresh
mellow	melodious	pleasing	pure
refreshing	luscious	angelic	savory
engaging	winning	winsome	delectable
delicious			

• •

SWIFT *(adjective)*

capable of quick motion; acting with readiness.

Optional Words:

brisk	fast	fleet	quick
rapid	speedy	hurriedly	expedite
rushed	velocity		

• • • • • • • • • • • • • •

T

Section Index

T

T

TACT *(noun)*

a quick or intuitive appreciation of what is fit, proper, or right; fine or ready discernment shown in saying or ding the proper thing.

Optional Words
cleverness   adroitness

TALENT *(noun)*

special or great ability; a particular and uncommon aptitude for special work or activity; people who have this.

Optional Words:

flair	**endowment**	**forte**	**aptness**
skill	**genius**	**expertise**	

TALK *(verb)*

to put ideas into spoken words; to speak or converse; to express ideas by speech.

Optional Words:

confer	**inform**	**consult**	**discuss**
discourse	**utter**	**rap**	**verbalize**
chat	**voice**	**vocalize**	**banter**
tell	**express**	**babble**	**communicate**
gab	**spout**		

TANGIBLE *(adjective)*

able to be perceived by touch; clear and definite; real.

Optional Words:

bodily	**physical**	**palpable**	**substantial**
material			

T

. . . .

TASTE *(noun)*

ability to perceive and enjoy what is beautiful or harmonious or to know what is fitting for an occasion; style or form with respect to the rules of propriety; individual preference.

Optional Words:

relish	refinement	tact	appreciation
grace			

TENACIOUS *(adjective)*

holding or clinging firmly to something (e.g. rights or principles).

Optional Words:

determined	persistent	tough	persevering
obstinate	stalwart	stout	steadfast
sturdy	true	viscous	bulldoggish
firm	strong	persisting	pertinacious
fixed			

TERRIFIC *(adjective)*

of great size or intensity; excellent.

Optional Words:

tremendous	sensational	splendid	wonderful
great	divine	marvelous	groovy
superb	glorious	amazing	swell

TESTIMONIAL *(noun)*

a formal statement testifying to a person's character, abilities or qualifications; something given to a person to show appreciation for his or her services or achievements.

Optional Words:

attestation	evidence	testament	recommendation
confirmation	appreciation	salute	commemoration
tribute	verification	substantiation	

THANKFUL *(adjective)*

feeling or expressing gratitude; deeply sensible of favors received.

Optional Words:

grateful	obliged	beholden	acknowledged
indebted to	obligated	appreciative	

THOROUGH *(adjective)*

complete in every way; persevering.

Optional Words:

exhaustive	detailed	particular	itemized
perfect	whole-hog	entire	full
sweeping	absolute		

T

THOUGHTFUL *(adjective)*

thinking deeply.

Optional Words:

reflective	attentive	circumspect	contemplative
analytical	meditative		

(adjective)

showing thought for the needs of others; considerate.

Optional Words:

chivalrous	attentive	heedful	mindful
concerned	earnest	observant	regardful
gallant	courteous	gracious	

TOP *(noun)*

the highest rank or degree; the highest or most honorable position; the utmost degree of intensity.

Optional Words:

maximum	crest	peak	zenith
summit	vertex	crown	culmination
cusp	head	point	tip
pinnacle			

TRANQUIL *(adjective)*

calm; quiet and motionless.

Optional Words:

sedate	serene	solemn	thoughtful
demure	collected	placid	easy
composed	poised	still	peaceful
stable	irenic	steady	

TRANSFORM *(verb)*

to make a great change in appearance or character.

Optional Words:

convert	alter	change	revolutionize
mutate	transfer	transmogrify	

TRANSMIT *(verb)*

to send or pass on from one person, place or thing to another.

Optional Words:

convey	send	remit	consign
route	transport	import	ship
traject	funnel		

TRANSPARENT *(adjective)*

easily understood or perceived; clear and unmistakable.

Optional Words:

candid	plain	evident	recognizable
articulate	crystal-clear	clear-cut	distinguishable
lucent	luminous	distinct	comprehensible
explicit	vivid		

T

························

TREASURE *(noun)*
a highly valued object; a beloved or highly valued person.
Optional Words:

prize	catch	plum	bonanza
lover	sweetheart	darling	

(verb)
to value highly.
Optional Words:

cherish	prize	esteem	guard
hold	dear	idolize	revere

TREMENDOUS *(adjective)*
immense.
Optional Words:

colossal	gigantic	huge	formidable
mighty	vast	enormous	

(adjective)
excellent.
Optional Words:

amazing	remarkable	terrific	extraordinary
astounding			

TRENDY *(adjective)*
up to date; following the latest trends of fashion.
Optional Words:

voguish	fashionable	swank	stylish

T

TRIER *(noun)*

a person who tries hard; one who always does his or her best.

Optional Words:
attempter

TRIM *(adjective)*

neat and orderly; having a smooth outline or compact structure.

Optional Words:

snug	**immaculate**	**spruce**	**methodical**
tidy	**streamlined**	**fit**	**well-groomed**
shipshape			

(verb)
to make neat or smooth.

Optional Words:

adjust	**fit**	**accommodate**

TRUE *(adjective)*

in accordance with; loyal; faithful to fact or reality.

Optional Words:

steadfast	**trustful**	**honest**	**constant**
resolute	**staunch**	**genuine**	**upright**
honorable	**sincere**	**credible**	

TRULY *(adverb)*

truthfully; sincerely; genuinely; faithfully.

Optional Words:

veritable	**indeed**	**positively**	**very**
actually	**absolutely**	**even**	**really**
surely	**loyally**	**decidedly**	**purely**

T

TRUST *(noun)*

firm belief in the reliability, truth or strength of a person or thing; confident expectation; responsibility arising from trust placed in an authority figure.

Optional Words:

credence	assurance	faith	presumption
confidence	conviction	certainty	

(verb)

to have or place trust in; to treat as reliable; to entrust.

Optional Words:

rely (on)	depend (on)	bank (on)	count (on)
presume			

TRUSTWORTHY *(adjective)*

worthy of trust; reliable.

Optional Words:

scrupulous	credible	honest	sincere
faithful	staunch	authentic	convincing
veracious	upright	secure	dependable
valid			

TRUTH *(noun)*

the quality of being true; something that is true.

Optional Words:

authenticity	veracity	fidelity	justice
virtue	honesty	integrity	exactness
gospel	truism	precision	

T

TRY *(verb)*

to attempt; to make an effort to do something.

Optional Words:
endeavor   undertake   aim   aspire
hope

(verb)
to test.

Optional Words:
examine   check   inspect   appraise
judge   weigh   experiment   prove

TUNE *(verb)*

to put in tune.

Optional Words:
attune   perform

(verb)
to adjust to run smoothly; to adopt to a particular tone,
expression or mood; to bring into harmony or accord.

Optional Words:
conform   coordinate   reconcile   accommodate
regulate   adjust

TWINKLE *(verb)*

to be bright or sparkling with amusement.

Optional Words:
glimmer   glitter   sparkle   flash
flicker   illuminate   shine   gleam
glint   glisten   shimmer   wink
blink   scintillate

T

TYPIFY *(verb)*

to be a representative specimen of.

Optional Words:

symbolize	embody	exemplify	characterize
personify	illustrate	mirror	emblematize
model			

U

Section Index

U

ULTIMATE *(adjective)*

beyond which there is no other; of the greatest size or significance; final, fundamental or essential.

Optional Words:

farthest	extreme	best	epitome
preeminent	towering	last	transcendent
closing	surpassing	absolute	categorical
grand	lofty	supreme	incomparable
elemental	utmost	maximum	

ULTRA *(adjective)*

going beyond the bounds of the moderation; extreme or extravagant.

Optional Words:

surpassing	excessive	outlandish	revolutionary
far-out	outré	outrageous	incomparable
preposterous			

UNDERSTAND *(verb)*

to perceive the meaning, importance or nature of; to know the ways or workings of; to know how to deal with; to become aware from information received; to draw as a conclusion.

Optional Words:

perceive	know	solve	comprehend
fathom	grasp	appreciate	cognize
conceive	conclude	deduce	experience
surmise	infer		

U

UNDERSTANDING *(adjective)*

having or showing insight, good judgment or sympathy towards others' feelings and points of view.

Optional Words:

intellectual	keen	discerning	compassionate
judicious	congenial	sympathetic	

(noun)

the power of thought, intelligence or ability to understand; the ability to show insight or feel sympathy; kindly tolerance; harmony in opinion or feeling.

Optional Words:

intellect	wisdom	perception	comprehension
reason	judgment	insight	discernment
sense	intuition	awareness	

UNDERTAKE *(verb)*

to agree or promise to do something.

Optional Words:

endeavor	strive	try	assay
attempt	venture		

(verb)

to make oneself responsible.

Optional Words:

pledge	promise	shoulder	devote

(verb)

to begin.

Optional Words:

commence	start	engage	launch

U

UNION *(noun)*

uniting or being united; a whole formed by uniting parts; an association formed by the uniting of people or groups.

Optional Words:

alliance	fusion	coalition	combination
melding	merger	association	junction
affiliation	meeting	connection	annexation
attachment	coming together		

UNIQUE *(adjective)*

being the only one of its kind.

Optional Words:

unusual	remarkable	rare	unprecedented
matchless	peerless	exceptional	extraordinary
sole	individual	singular	incomparable
novel			

UNISON *(noun)*

sounding or singing together at the same pitch or a corresponding one.

Optional Words:

harmony	concert	concord	consonance
melody	homophony		

(noun)

in agreement or accord.

Optional Words:

unity	concord	conjunction	symphony
alliance			

U

UNITE *(verb)*

to join together; to make or become one; to agree, combine or cooperate.

Optional Words:

merge	consolidate	blend	cohere
compound	conjoin	connect	fuse
mix	link	bond	associate
marry	relate	affiliate	concur
ally	mingle	weld	

UNITY *(noun)*

the state of being one or a unit; a thing forming a complex whole.

Optional Words:

solidarity	harmony	concord	homogeneity
rapport	agreement	oneness	congruity
integration			

UNIVERSAL *(adjective)*

of, for or done by all.

Optional Words:

ubiquitous	general	generic	omnipresent
common	total	widespread	comprehensive
extensive	vast	entire	prevalent
usual	whole	sweeping	

U

UP *(adverb)*

to, in or at a higher place, level, value or condition; to a larger size.

Optional Words:

aloft	above	overhead	over
upwards			

UPGRADE *(verb)*

to raise to a higher grade or rank.

Optional Words:

boost	advance	elevate	promote
increase			

UPHOLD *(verb)*

to support; to support a decision, statement or belief.

Optional Words:

bolster	advocate	champion	endorse
abet	aid	assent	help
preserve	justify	buoy	sustain
elevate	uplift		

UPKEEP *(noun)*

keeping something in good condition and repair; the cost of this.

Optional Words:

preservation	maintenance	support	sustentation
conservation			

U

UPLIFT *(verb)*

to raise; to mentally or morally elevate.

Optional Words:

exhilarate	inspire	heighten	elevate
hoist	raise	improve	irradiate
erect	heave	advance	ascend
increase	better	cultivate	enhance

UPPER *(adjective)*

higher in place or position; ranking above others.

Optional Words:

superior	better than	lofty	apical
highest	top	topmost	above
overhead			

UPRIGHT *(adjective)*

strictly honest or honorable.

Optional Words:

ethical	good	honest	just
moral	pure	virtuous	worthy
righteous	fair	impartial	circumspect
correct	principled		

UPSTANDING *(adjective)*

standing upright.

Optional Words:
raised

(adjective)
moral.

Optional Words:

honest	**genuine**	**honorable**	**conscientious**
credible	**sincere**	**reliable**	**straightforward**
scrupulous			

URGE *(verb)*

to drive onward; to encourage to proceed; to recommend strongly with reasoning.

Optional Words:

persuade	**plead**	**pique**	**prompt**
spur	**coax**	**incite**	**solicit**
press	**motivate**		

URGENT *(adjective)*

needing immediate attention, action or decision.

Optional Words:

compelling	**crucial**	**imperative**	**pressing**
burning	**impelling**	**driving**	**exigent**
insistent	**essential**	**vital**	

U

USE *(noun)*

the right or power of using something.

Optional Words:

benefit	profit	worth	service
utility	usefulness	efficacy	efficiency
adequacy	utilization	function	applicability

UTMOST *(adjective)*

furthest, greatest or extreme.

Optional Words:

paramount	primary	farthest	furthermost
maximum	top	topmost	ultimate
chief	entire	whole	full
complete	total	absolute	highest

UTOPIA *(noun)*

an imaginary place or state of things where everything is perfect; a visionary scheme for social improvement.

Optional Words:

Arcadia	Heaven	paradise	wonderland
Zion	Shangri-la		

V

Section Index

V

VALENTINE *(noun)*

a sweetheart chosen on Saint Valentine's Day; a greeting card or token of affection given on Saint Valentine's Day.

Optional Words:

missive	card	love	verse
letter			

VALUE *(noun)*

the amount of money, other commodity or service considered to be equivalent to something else or for which a thing can be exchanged.

Optional Words:

desirability	usefulness	importance	worth
account	valuation	estimate	rate
figure			

VARIOUS *(adjective)*

of several kinds; unlike one another; more than one; individual and separate.

Optional Words:

diverse	myriad	many	variegated
different	distinct	separate	individual
several	sundry	some	disparate
variable	multiple		

VENERABLE *(adjective)*

worthy of deep respect because of age or associations.

Optional Words:

honorable	esteemed	revered	honored
hallowed	revered	respected	stately
admirable	estimable	worshipful	sacred
idolized	dignified	imposing	ancient
old	grand	sage	wise

V

· ·

VERACIOUS *(adjective)*

truthful, true or accurate.

Optional Words:

factual	faithful	valid	sincere
correct	actual	trustworthy	honest
just	right		

VERBATIM *(adverb & adjective)*

in exactly the same words; word-for-word.

Optional Words:

directly	literally	accurately	precisely
exactly	literatim	literal	accurate
precise	exact		

VERGE *(noun)*

the point beyond which something new begins or occurs.

Optional Words:

brink	threshold	brim	edge
fringe	border	margin	terminus

VERITY *(noun)*

the truth of something.

Optional Words:

truth	honesty	gospel	verisimilitude
truism	actuality	reality	

V

VERVE *(noun)*

enthusiasm, liveliness and vigor.

Optional Words:

energy	spirit	spring	gusto
oomph	life	bounce	zest
fire	animation	brio	dash
élan	vim	vivacity	

VERY *(adverb)*

in a high degree; extremely; in the fullest sense; exactly.

Optional Words:

authentically	indubitably	genuinely	really
truly	exactly	precisely	exceedingly
ideally	decidedly	notably	greatly
acutely	positively	emphatically	

VIBRANT *(adjective)*

vibrating or resonant; thrilling with energy or activity.

Optional Words:

dynamic	energetic	vigorous	plangent
resounding	ringing	vivacious	

VICTORY *(noun)*

success in a contest or game.

Optional Words:

mastery	conquest	supremacy	achievement
triumph	win	dominion	accomplished
superiority	upper hand		

V

····························

VIEW *(noun)*

a mental attitude.

Optional Words:

conviction	belief	thought	opinion
feeling	persuasion	sentiment	perspection
concept	deduction	inference	position
stand			

(verb)

to regard or consider.

Optional Words:

see	behold	discern	perceive
eye	recognize	observe	contemplate

VIGIL *(noun)*

a period of staying awake to keep watch or pray.

Optional Words:

lookout	watch	attention	surveillance
sentry	wakefulness		

VIGOR *(noun)*

active physical or mental strength; energy; flourishing
physical condition.

Optional Words:

drive	getup	spirit	exuberance
pep	punch	push	snap
vitality	steam		

•••••••••••••••••

V

VIRILE *(adjective)*

having strength or vigor; having procreative power.

Optional Words:

sturdy	intrepid	robust	driving
strong	energetic	forceful	vigorous
potent			

VIRTUE *(noun)*

moral excellence or goodness; a particular form of this; chastity; a good quality; an advantage.

Optional Words:

rectitude	honesty	honor	faithfulness
integrity	justice	purity	probity
goodness	ideal	ethic	righteousness
prudence	excellence	value	fortitude

VISION *(noun)*

imaginative insight into a subject or problem; foresight and wisdom in planning.

Optional Words:

revelation	apocalypse	oracle	prophecy
apparition	daydream	dream	phenomenon
fantasy			

(noun)

a person or sight of unusual beauty.

Optional Words:

presence	apparition	phenomenon

V

VIVACIOUS *(adjective)*

lively and high-spirited.

Optional Words:

buoyant	ebullient	exuberant	effervescent
brisk	animated	cheerful	frolicsome
merry	alert	gay	keen
sprightly	zesty	playful	

VIVID *(adjective)*

bright and strong; intense; producing strong and clear mental pictures; creating ideas in an active and lively way.

Optional Words:

vibrant	brilliant	clear	resplendent
keen	luminous	quick	colorful
gay	acute	intense	lively
spirited	sharp	expressive	rich
animated			

VOICE *(verb)*

to put into words; to express.

Optional Words:

articulate	verbalize	vocalize	present
recount	tell	utter	vent
express	state	speak	

VOLUNTARY *(adjective)*

acting, done or given of one's own free will; working or done without payment.

Optional Words:

optional	gratuitous	willing	enthusiastic
unasked	spontaneous		

V

VOTE *(noun)*

a formal expression of one's opinion or choice on a matter under discussion; an opinion or choice expressed in this way.

Optional Words:

ballot	election	poll	voice
selection			

VOUCH *(verb)*

to guarantee the certainty, accuracy or reliability of.

Optional Words:

assure	guarantee	endorse	authenticate
warrant	attest	affirm	substantiate
promise	bond	vow	corroborate
certify	state	witness	agree

VOW *(noun)*

a solemn promise or undertaking, especially in the form of an oath to God or a saint.

Optional Words:

pledge	troth	contract	oath
covenant	promise	assertion	declaration

W

W

W

WANT *(verb)*

to desire; to wish for.

Optional Words:

crave	prefer	aspire	hanker
incline	fancy	long	

WARM *(adjective)*

enthusiastic; hearty; a vigorous response; kindly and affectionate.

Optional Words:

keen	zealous	tender	passionate
affable	kindhearted	responsive	wholehearted
softhearted	sincere	ardent	compassionate
fervent	cordial	gracious	sympathetic

WARRANTY *(noun)*

a guarantee.

Optional Words:

pledge	surety	bond	authorization
assurance	testimony		

WATCH *(verb)*

to safeguard; to exercise protective care, give earnest heed or be observant.

Optional Words:

tend	lookout	mind	see
ward	mark	follow	behold
discern	attend	notice	regard
chaperon			

WEALTH *(noun)*

riches; possession of riches.

Optional Words:

affluence	comfort	fortune	independence
funds	opulence	property	treasures
substance	prosperity	means	possessions
assets	capital	resources	estate
goods	holdings		

(noun)
a great quantity.

Optional Words:

abundance	plenty	mass	multitude
heap	volume		

WEALTHY *(adjective)*

rich.

Optional Words:

opulent	affluent	well-to-do	moneyed
comfortable	prosperous	well-off	well-healed
auspicious			

(adjective)
abundant.

Optional Words:

profligate	lavish	profuse	resplendent
sufficient	enough	ample	plentiful
copious	abounding	replete	plentious
flush	luxurious	bountiful	

W

WED *(verb)*

to unite.

Optional Words:

combine	join	pledge	associate
conjoin	connect	link	marry
yoke	relate	splice	

WELCOME *(adjective)*

received with pleasure.

Optional Words:

desirable	honored	esteemed	appreciated
agreeable			

WELL *(adverb)*

in a good or suitable way; according to one's wishes.

Optional Words:

agreeably	delightfully	rightly	satisfactorily
thoroughly	carefully	favorably	advantageously
kindly	beneficially		

WHIMSICAL *(adjective)*

playful; fanciful; quaint.

Optional Words:

amusing	fantastic	delightful	light-hearted
comical	capricious	funny	quizzical
extravagant			

W

WHIRL *(noun)*

a whirling movement; a bustling activity.

Optional Words:

spin	pirouette	twirl	whirligig
swirl	eddy	turn	hurry
speed	whiz	reel	whisk
flurry	gyration		

WHISK *(verb)*

to move with a quick, light, sweeping movement; to go rapidly.

Optional Words:

hurry	barrel	flit	fly
speed	zig	whip	flutter

WHIZ *(verb)*

to make a sound like that of a speeding object.

Optional Words:

hiss	buzz	fizz	fizzle
sizzle	swish	wheeze	whoosh
whisper			

(verb)
to move very quickly.

Optional Words:

hurry	speed

(noun)
an exceptionally brilliant or successful young person.

Optional Words:

expert	adept	master	professional
virtuoso			

. . . .

WHOLE *(noun)*

the full or complete amount.

Optional Words:

mass	aggregate	collective	total
entirety	sum	bulk	gross

WILL *(noun)*

the power of conscious; deliberate action; the faculty by which the mind makes choices and acts to carry them out.

Optional Words:

wish	fancy	inclination	pleasure
discipline	passion	intent	restraint
choice	volition	purpose	self-command
desire			

WIN *(verb)*

to be victorious in; to gain a victory; to gain the favor or support of.

Optional Words:

overcome	prevail	triumph	conquer
gain	accomplish	achieve	attain
rack up	realize	score	earn
acquire	produce	secure	get
procure			

WINSOME *(adjective)*

having an engagingly attractive appearance or manner.

Optional Words:

charming	persuasive	pleasing	attractive
joyous	amiable	lovely	sweet
dulcet	adorable	lovable	cute

. . . .

W

WISDOM *(noun)*

being wise; soundness of judgment; a wise saying; common sense.

Optional Words:

erudition	acumen	depth	enlightenment
capacity	foresight	insight	judiciousness
learning	sage	knowing	discernment
intelligence	command		

WISH *(verb)*

to have or express as a wish; to hope or express hope about another person's welfare.

Optional Words:

expect	hope	fancy	want
crave	will	choose	elect
like			

WIT *(noun)*

the ability to combine words or ideas ingeniously so as to produce a kind of clever humor that appeals to the intellect.

Optional Words:

repartee	fun	playfulness	jest
banter	delight		

(noun)

intelligence and understanding.

Optional Words:

astuteness	acumen	mind	clear-sightedness
grasp	sense	keenness	perception
brilliance	insight	intelligent	comprehension
brain	awareness		

WIZARD *(noun)*

a person with amazing abilities.

Optional Words:

prodigy	**genius**	**virtuoso**	**magician**
expert	**artist**	**authority**	**master**
whiz			

WONDER *(noun)*

a feeling of surprise mingled with admiration; curiosity.

Optional Words:

awe	**amazement**	**sensation**	**bewilderment**
fascination	**surprise**	**astonishment**	

(noun)

marvel; a remarkable thing or event.

Optional Words:

prodigy	**miracle**	**curiosity**	**phenomenon**
spectacle			

WOO *(verb)*

to try to achieve or obtain; to seek the favor of; to try to coax or persuade.

Optional Words:

solicit	**pursue**	**invite**	**address**
court			

W

WORK *(noun)*

that upon which labor is extended; the acts or obligation that one does or undertakes in return for something of value, as money (especially the activities by which one earns one's livelihood); occupation.

Optional Words:

business	job	calling	employment
line	pursuit	art	craft
trade	profession	duty	labor
effort	vocation		

WORTH *(noun)*

having a specified value; a satisfactory or rewarding return; wealth.

Optional Words:

virtue	value	merit	significance
usefulness	quality		

WOW *(interjection)*

an exclamation of astonishment or admiration.

(noun slang)
a sensational success.

(verb slang)
to impress or excite greatly.

Section Index

YES
YIPPEE
YOUTHFUL
YULE
YUMMY

Y

Defined Words and Options
Page 508

Y

YES *(adverb)*

it is so; the statement is correct.

Optional Words:

aye	OK	yea	certainly
gladly	willingly	exactly	by all means
precisely			

YIPPEE *(interjection)*

an exclamation of excitement.

Optional Words:

wow	hallelujah	hooray	hurrah

YOUTHFUL *(adjective)*

young; looking or seeming young.

Optional Words:

fresh	energetic	childlike	bright-eyed
adolescent	vigorous	buoyant	light-hearted
full-of-life	limber	bubbling	

YULE *(noun)*

of or having to do with the season surrounding the celebration of the birth of Christ.

Optional Words:

nativity	Christmas Season	Christmastide

Y

YUMMY *(adjective)*

tasty and delicious; gratifying to the senses, especially taste.

Optional Words:

delightful	ambrosial	delectable	scrumptious
heavenly	luscious	sumptuous	

Z

Z

Z

ZANY *(noun)*

a comical or eccentric person.

Optional Words:

harlequin	funnyman	comedian	humorist
farceur	cutup	joker	wag
clown	comic	wit	

(adjective)
crazily funny.

Optional Words:

hilarious	comic	merry	vivacious
mirthful	rollicking		

ZEAL *(noun)*

enthusiasm; hearty and persistent effort.

Optional Words:

zest	ardor	fervor	passion
fire	energy	gusto	readiness
intensity	spirit	eagerness	keenness

ZEST *(noun)*

keen enjoyment or interest; pleasantly stimulating quality.

Optional Words:

gusto	passion	zeal	verve
heart	relish	ardor	eagerness
enthusiasm	fervor	delight	ecstasy
enjoyment	pleasure	cheer	happiness

Z

ZING *(noun)*

vigor or energy.

Optional Words:

eagerness	**ardor**	**spirit**	**enthusiasm**
animation	**brio**	**dash**	**élan**
life	**oomph**	**vim**	**verve**
zip			

(verb)

to move swiftly.

Optional Words:

speed	**hurry**	**streak**	**zip**
dash			

ZIP *(noun)*

energy, vigor and liveliness.

Optional Words:

eagerness	**ardor**	**spirit**	**enthusiasm**
animation	**brio**	**élan**	**oomph**
vim	**verve**		

ZOOM *(verb)*

to move or rise quickly.

Optional Words:

skyrocket	**soar**	**bolt**	**streak**
speed	**rush**	**zip**	**dash**
hurry			

Most Often Used Words

Most Often Used Words

Section Index

ABILITY	HONEST
ADVOCATE	IMPORTANT
AFFECTION	IMPRESS
ATTRACTIVE	IMPROVE
BEST	INCENTIVE
BRAVE	JOIN
CELEBRATE	LARGE
CELEBRATION	LEAD
CHEER	LEARN
COMBINE	LIGHT
CREATIVE	LUCK
DECENT	NEW
DEVOTED	NICE
DISCOVER	PLAN
DYNAMIC	POSITIVELY
EXCITEMENT	POWERFUL
FANCY	PRAISE
FANTASY	PRODUCE
FANTASTIC	PROFITABLE
FEELING	PROMOTE
FORTUNE	PROTECT
FOUNDATION	REGARD
FRIEND	RIGHT
GENEROUS	SPEED
GROW	STRONG
GUARANTEE	SUCCEED
HARMONIOUS	TALK
HONESTY	WEALTHY

ABILITY *(noun)*

ableness

capability

capacity

competence

faculty

might

adeptness

command

edified

enlightened

expertise

expertness

guided

knack

know-how

mastery

proficiency

skill

aptitude

talent

cognizant

wise

mindful

scholarly

lore

date

facto

bright

clever

knowing

sharp

discovering

Gnostic

perceptive

sage

profound

savant

ADVOCATE *(verb)*

support	fortify	brace
favor	strengthen	sustain
recommend	back	maintain
help	reinforce	adhere
bolster	verify	champion
assist	affirm	expounder
hand	buoy	proponent
defend	advance	uphold
lift	bank on	side (with)
succor	depend	endorse
preserve	push	approve
aid	relief	applaud
corroborate	carry	favor
substantiate	trust	pull (for)
confirm	devote	embrace
finance	comfort	provide (for)
cheer	secours	encourage

AFFECTION *(noun)*

fondness	devotion	charming
liking	bond	cherished
love	loyalty	close
fancy	tie	intimate
attachment	respect	precious
friendship	esteem	committed
influence	regard	promised
worship	admiration	veracious
delight in	amazement	solicitation
idolize	darling	true
revere	dear	dedication
venerate	favorite	caring
groove on	sweetheart	

ATTRACTIVE *(adjective)*

alluring	pleasing	awesome
appealing	appearance	impressive
attracting	flattering	overwhelming
captivating	correct	stunning
charming	beguiling	ethereal
enchanting	amusing	delicate
fascinating	celebrated	delectable
magnetic	dignified	elegant
tempting	famous	tasteful
winning	great	graceful
winsome	desirable	gracious
pleasureful	refined	luxurious
beautiful	worthy	suave
pretty	dainty	sophisticated
fine	delectable	scrumptious
handsome	exquisite	intriguing
gorgeous	dazzle	enthralling
belle	amazing	interesting
becoming	astounding	

BEST *(adjective)*

basic	superior	prestigious
initial	supreme	choice
leading	ultimate	first
main	ideal	finest
original	highest	top
paramount	quintessential	prime
preeminent	greatest	excellent
primary	transcendent	noblest
principal	loftiest	crowning
chief	dominant	premium
foremost	eminent	

BRAVE *(adjective)*

intrepid	chivalrous	resolute
bold	noble	spirited
confident	spunky	steadfast
courageous	audacious	helpful
daring	doughty	heart
gallant	gusty	strong
heroic	lionhearted	tenacious
game	stalwart	venturous
stouthearted	stout	mighty
valiant	valorous	powerful
venturesome	gritty	herolike
vigorous	hardy	

CELEBRATE *(verb)*

acclaim

regard

recognize

extol

applaud

praise

honor

glorify

cheer

commend

hail

kudize

bless

commemorate

eulogize

admire

consecrate

worship

acknowledgment

exalt

fete

ceremonialize

sanctify

dedicate

signalize

hallow

lionize

inaugurate

laud

duplicate

rite

observe

act

beatify

rejoice

revel

revere

ritualize

solemnize

venerate

keep

proclaim

memorialize

CELEBRATION *(noun)*

carnival
fair
feast
gala
holiday
jamboree
jubilee
festivity
party
fete

banquet
festival
assembly
merrymaking
commemoration
glorification
magnification
laudation
anniversary

ceremonial
solemnization
keeping
observance
merriment
occasion
happening
occurrence
fiesta

TO CHEER *(verb)*

amuse	enthrall	hearten
pleasure	fascinate	adore
charm	gladden	gratify

CHEER *(noun)*

triumph	mirth	joy
gaiety	revelry	happiness
merrymaking	vivacity	fancy
frivolity	festivity	charm
jollity	glee	enjoyment
joviality	merriment	

CHEER *(adjective)*

embolden	elated	blithe
enhearten	eager	lithesome
felicity	animated	lively
light-hearted	delightful	carefree
nice	bright	gay
exhilarated	radiant	congenial
joyful	sunny	

COMBINE *(verb)*

interact	wed	cooperate
intermingle	fuse	merge
interconnect	amalgamate	pool
interface	commingle	coincide
join	blend	affiliate
associate	consolidate	hook-up
coalesce	unify	partner
connect	embody	synthesize
relate	integrate	mix
unite		

CREATIVE *(adjective)*

original

ingenious

innovative

inventive

novel

constructive

formative

inceptive

incipient

beginning

fresh

new

different

unique

unusual

special

preliminary

DECENT *(adjective)*

tasteful	seemly	gracious
good	standard	modest
adequate	chaste	nice
presentable	ethical	satisfactory
kind	spotless	suitable
right	prudent	sufficient
noble	mannerly	polite
comfortable	virtuous	good
generous	acceptable	adequate
conforming	pure	respectable
all right	proper	correct
appropriate	accommodating	desired
apt	fair	precise
fitting	just	accordant
straight-laced	courteous	tasteful
obliging	customary	

DEVOTED *(adjective)*

zealous

committed

intense

consigned

allotted

assigned

consecrated

dedicated

affirmed

assured

dutiful

pledged

faithful

loyal

confirmed

given

vowed

conscientious

ardent

constant

resolute

staunch

steadfast

steady

dependable

reliable

trustworthy

attached

attentive

solicitous

bound

DISCOVER *(verb)*

comprehend	learn	note
detect	reveal	observe
realize	disclose	perceive
understand	locate	learn
ascertain	divulge	invent
determine	grasp	recognize
find out	realize	ferret out
find	notice	root out
see	encounter	sense
unearth	spot	feel
get	discern	

DYNAMIC *(adjective)*

energetic	vibrant	dramatic
zealous	tough	stirring
active	vigorous	progressive
spirited	mighty	spectacular
appealing	vital	electric
exuberant	authoritative	striking
charismatic	explosive	high powered
driving	commanding	peppy
forceful	exciting	efficacious
robust	impressive	fervent
magnetic	sensational	ardent
able	compelling	efficient
powerful	thrilling	electrified
dominant	assertive	astonishing

EXCITEMENT *(noun)*

action	provocation	ardor
hubbub	commotion	eagerness
excitedness	flurry	zealousness
enthusiasm	bustle	earnestness
stir	to-do	intensity
movement	animation	keenness
excitation	exhilaration	vim
emotion	passion	ardency
stimulation	flutter	ecstasy
drama	bustle	vivacity
melodrama	joyfulness	impetuosity

FANCY *(adjective)*

decorative
intricate
ornate
elaborate
ornamental
trimmed
garnished
embellished
enhanced
graced
adorned
bedecked
beautified

decked out
tasteful
refined
dignified
charming
debonair
cultivated
exquisite
graceful
gracious
luxurious
suave
scrumptious

frilly
rich
stylish
extravagant
flamboyant
baroque
opulent
gilded
enriched
beautiful
spruced up
dandified
furbished

FANTASY *(noun)*

daydream
envisagement
fancy
awareness
reverie
whim
dream
fabrication
aspiration

fiction
desire
invention
vision
conception
wish
thought
chimera

delusion
mirage
revelation
phantasm
phenomenon
visualization
apparition
illusion

FANTASTIC *(noun)*

remarkable	extraordinary	priceless
excellent	glorious	peerless
great	grand	rare
extreme	wonderful	neat
extravagant	miraculous	keen
fabulous	amazing	masterful
incredible	awesome	classy
marvelous	colossal	unusual
phenomenal	formidable	astonishing
tremendous	exquisite	premium
distinguished	fine	choice
eminent	matchless	great
heroic	sublime	prime
huge	superior	select
majestic	large	desirable
magnificent	extensive	world-class
monumental	towering	first-class
outstanding	vital	striking
prominent	foremost	paramount
superb	exemplary	notable
transcendent	terrific	great
weighty	tops	

Most Often Used Words

FEELING *(noun)*

empathy
sensation
sensitivity
affection
thought
sympathy
commiseration
grace
belief
feel
sensory
sensitiveness
response
perception

perceptiveness
susceptibility
consciousness
receptivity
responsiveness
excitability
excitement
motility
impressibility
keenness
spirit
delicacy
pathos
awareness

attitude
capacity
faculty
intuition
sense
impression
conviction
sentiment
compassion
affinity
rapport
appreciation
understanding

FORTUNE *(noun)*

affluence

goods

holdings

bonanza

bundle

windfall

assets

resources

worth

inheritance

bounty

capital

mint

well-off

prosperity

property

providence

substance

success

wealth

riches

possessions

abundance

comfort

funds

opulence

plenty

treasure

FOUNDATION *(noun)*

base	essence	establishment
basis	inauguration	formulation
beginning	origination	constitution
groundwork	source	organization
infrastructure	bedrock	start up
justification	footing	understructure
substructure	ground	substratum
support	underpinning	

FRIEND *(noun)*

ally	adherent	alter ego
running mate	coworker	helper
buddy	protector	associate
amigo	attendant	mate
intimate	comrade	fellow
copartner	confederate	counterpart
companion	running mate	partner
disciple	confidant	cohort
partisan	disciple	confrere
compatriot	pal	colleague
fast friend	patron	chum
sidekick	benefactor	crony
accomplice		

GENEROUS *(adjective)*

beneficent	willing	tender
charitable	bounteous	merciful
giving	munificent	lenient
benevolent	openhanded	indulgent
considerate	benign	affable
great-hearted	humane	good-natured
magnanimous	humanitarian	obliging
altruistic	philanthropic	gentle
thoughtful	compassionate	genial
fair	responsive	amiable
helpful	warm	sweet-tempered

GROW *(verb)*

change	spiral	succeed
enlarge	swell	develop
swell	build up	raise
beef up	thrive	produce
build	accelerate	propagate
flourish	quicken	cultivate
boost	further	expand
elevate	compound	bloom
heighten	flower	augment
burgeon	upgrade	multiply
mount	glorify	amplify
dilate	blossom	progress
inflate	snowball	advance
aggrandize	push	move up
exalt	increase	unfold
hike	run up	improve
enhance	magnify	develop
yield	maximize	enrich
foster	dramatize	gain
escalate	prosper	

GUARANTEE *(noun)*

warranty
surety
promise
bond
word
oath
vow

assurance
token
good faith
conviction
confidence
sureness
patronage

security
covenant
testimony
pact
compactly
deed

TO GUARANTEE *(verb)*

stand behind
endorse
justify
assure
secure
back
sponsor
affirm
swear
assert

declare
attest
witness
uphold
corroborate
prove
substantiate
verify
contract
agree

concur
authenticate
aver
vouch for
answer
stand behind
pledge
evince
make certain

HARMONIOUS *(adjective)*

agreeable	unified	like
appropriate	in concert	peaceful
compatible	congenial	consonant
complimentary	fit	corresponding
fluent	suitable	adapted
harmonic	conforming	amicable
mellifluous	congruent	co-operative
melodious	accordant	in step
synchronized	concordant	consistent
symmetric	similar	

HONESTY *(noun)*

virtue	credence	constancy
goodness	verity	trustiness
integrity	rectitude	responsibility
honor	uprightness	openness
justice	fidelity	frankness
purity	fairness	candor
probity	impeccability	truth
faithfulness	reliability	confidence
veracity	soundness	right
certainty		

HONEST *(adjective)*

true	authentic	correct
truthful	reliable	exact
trustworthy	scrupulous	intrinsic
straight-forward	credible	verifiable
candid	factual	respectable
ethical	faithful	plain
forthright	conscientious	sound
frank	genuine	veritable
honorable	legitimate	literal
sincere	authoritative	precise
upright	licit	realistic
virtuous	valid	reasonable
loyal	cogent	aboveboard
direct	telling	
just	well-founded	

IMPORTANT *(adjective)*

consequential
eminent
influential
major
meaningful
momentous
notable
prominent
significant
vital
big
considerable
material
substantial
weighty
marked
conspicuous
noteworthy
outstanding

powerful
valuable
worthwhile
worthy
first-class
first-rate
distinguished
famous
celebrated
exalted
preeminent
illustrious
famed
great
star
stellar
superior
extensive
hefty

remarkable
essential
critical
paramount
primary
foremost
principle
earnest
salient
serious
grave
relevant
necessary
urgent
well-known
extraordinary
powerful leading
incomparable

IMPRESS *(verb)*

affect	stamp	control
establish	sway	command
imprint	move	stand out
influence	touch	engage
instill	inspire	attention
mark	convince	fascinate
persuade	prevail over	dazzle
plant	awe	excite

IMPROVE *(verb)*

make better	adjust	upgrade
cultivate	grow	raise
enhance	refine	fix
enrich	edit	correct
amend	enlarge	rally
help	emend	widen
mend	change	increase
update	renew	mature
elevate	develop	lift
polish	better	

INCENTIVE *(noun)*

encouragement

impetus

inducement

motivation

provocation

stimulus

inspiration

spur

drive

exhortation

incitement

urge

enticement

motive

spring

purpose

ground

rationale

reason

influence

persuasion

instigation

impulse

JOIN *(verb)*

adhere	muster	piece (together)
affix	sign up	mix
associate	cooperate	lump
attach	integrate	append
connect	knit	entwine
consolidate	weave	interlace
fasten	bind	clamp
fuse	coalesce	weld
meet	conjoin	leash
merge	couple	annex
unite	link	intermix
abut	marry	pair (with)
enter	wed	border
enlist		

LARGE *(adjective)*

huge
big
wide
grand
great
considerable
substantial
vast
massive
gigantic
mountainous
extensive
immense
bulky
spacious
capacious
colossal

extended
plentiful
copious
ample
corpulent
obese
Herculean
titanic
monstrous
towering
mighty
magnificent
commodious
enormous
giant
jumbo

tremendous
prodigious
monumental
stupendous
voluminous
overgrown
ponderous
gargantuan
super
king-sized
blooming
whopping
hefty
major
husky
oversized

LEAD *(verb)*

conduct	shepherd	engineer
convey	show	channel
direct	usher	precede
guide	launch	squire
induce	embark	protect
manage	commence	guard
persuade	accompany	safeguard
pilot	chaperone	watch over
reign	attend	drive
rule	carry	command
steer	oversee	influence
escort	supervise	motivate
route	regulate	start

LEARN *(verb)*

absorb	reveal	surmount
comprehend	disclose	lick
determine	embody	overcome
realize	divulge	triumph
understand	engross	hurdle
ascertain	assimilate	notice
catch on	incorporate	encounter
find out	acquire	discern
hear	detect	note
see	find	observe
unearth	locate	perceive
get	grasp	read
pick up	master	peruse
study	memorize	pore over
unlock	conquer	

LIGHT *(noun)*

radiation	ray	splendor
brightness	flare	irradiation
beacon	lamp	resplendence
beam	emission	effulgence
blaze	incandescence	glimmer
brilliance	gleam	glitter
glow	glare	sparkle
illumination	flame	sheen
shine	luminosity	luster

LUCK *(noun)*

destiny
fate
kismet
fluke
fortuity
godsend
prosperity

weal
wealth
windfall
advantage
profit
triumph
victory

karma
win
opportunity
break
blessings

NEW *(adjective)*

different
just out
fresh
latest
modish
distinct
chic
contemporary
prevalent present
raw
novel
young

beginning
primary
original
prime
initial
opening
inaugural
recent
primeval
leading
just made

newly arrived
invented
discovered
current
faddish
fashionable
innovative
inventive
modern
of late
first

NICE *(adjective)*

pleasant	amiable	gracious
satisfactory	delightful	genial
agreeable	obliging	gentle
amicable	kind	decorous
congenial	kindly	becoming
respectable	helpful	modest
virtuous	delicate	demure
winning	fastidious	favorable
winsome	fine	good
cordial	marvelous	gratifying
courteous	proper	befitting
ingratiating	refined	decent
considerate	charming	seemly
cultured		

PLAN *(noun)*

aim	diagram	undertaking
intention	blueprint	projection
method	chart	procedure
order	conception	policy
pattern	design	plot
purpose	idea	stratagem
strategy	scheme	disposition
system	flow chart	

TO PLAN *(verb)*

invent	outline	contemplate
concoct	prepare	sketch
calculate	devise	put forth
map out	arrange	intend
organize	formulate	delineate

POSITIVELY *(adverb)*

certainly	decidedly	simply
precisely	correctly	truly
righteously	exactly	purely
genuinely	definitely	perfectly
ultimately	thoroughly	decisively
utterly	rigorously	categorically
clearly	expressly	explicitly
absolutely	conclusively	factually
strictly		

POWERFUL *(adjective)*

energetic	capable	in control
sturdy	strenuous	commanding
husky	dominant	omnipotent
zealous	vital	skillful
spirited	tough	masterful
exuberant	stout	gifted
robust	vigorous	dynamic
assured	competent	alive
vibrant	forceful	vitalized
strong	effective	lusty
wieldy	authoritative	intense
able	influential	

PRAISE *(noun)*

accolade	giving thanks	hand clapping
bravos	obeisance	plaudit
award	recognition	acclamation
kudos	endorsement	applause
extolling	tribute	cheering
adulation	elevation	greet
blandishment	aggrandize	honoring
esteem	admire	distinction
sycophancy	paean	advocacy
homage	blessing	cheers
rave over	approval	hurrahs
laudation	ovation	

TO PRAISE *(verb)*

commend	laud	sanctify
rudize	magnify	venerate
recommend	panegyrize	applaud
compliment	resound	adulate
glorify	distinguish	elevate
exalt	ennoble	aggrandize
celebrate	proclaim	cajole
cry up	intensify	admire
extol	boost	cheer
eulogize	plug	acclaim
adore	hallow	hail
bless	worship	salute
flatter	revere	honor

PRODUCE *(verb)*

accomplish	father	reproduce
assemble	fabricate	put together
cause	frame	put on
compose	form	originate
constitute	stage	blossom
create	give	produce
effect	grow	flower
exhibit	breed	deliver
furnish	cultivate	allow
generate	raise	admit
make	engender	contribute
manifest	spawn	proliferate
manufacture	induce	afford
present	muster (up)	return
propagate	hatch	render
show	multiply	come through
yield	bring about	offer
bear	beget	provide
turn out		

PROFITABLE *(adjective)*

gainful	useful	assisting
lucrative	prosperous	effective
moneymaking	propitious	pragmatic
paying	rich	practical
remunerative	substantial	instrumental
well-paying	sustaining	serviceable
worthwhile	self-sustaining	valuable
worthy	aiding	contributive
beneficial	successful	conducive
productive	favorable	

PROMOTE *(verb)*

further	benefit	advocate
forward	improve	cultivate
urge	aid	cooperate
encourage	assist	avail
nourish	develop	hype
nurture	support	improve
subsidize	back	push
subserve	favor	bolster
succor	expand	develop
profit	better	speed
patronize	boost	foster
help	uphold	boom
second	champion	bestead
befriend	advertise	plug

PROTECT *(verb)*

cover	shelter	preserve
buffer	watch	conserve
prevent	keep safe	hide
oppose	keep secure	withstand
defend	ward	resist
escort	safeguard	maintain
observe	save	fortify
patrol	harbor	support

REGARD *(noun)*

admiration

appreciation

attention

concern

consideration

esteem

honor

respect

solicitude

favor

deference

homage

approval

RIGHT *(adjective)*

accurate	seemly	genuine
actual	conforming	just
authentic	decent	moral
correct	true	precise
exact	undistorted	proper
exactly	fixed	suitable
upright	circumscribed	appropriate
valid	fitting	

SPEED *(noun)*

haste	alacrity	rapidity
clip	swiftness	velocity
urgency	dispatch	tempo
quickness	acceleration	celerity
pace	fast pace	
momentum		

TO SPEED *(verb)*

rush	whisk	hustle
rocket	move fast	highball
zip	charge	chase
whiz	expedite	tear

STRONG *(adjective)*

solid
established
fixed
anchored
definite
determined
moored
resolute
rigid
stable
staunch
steadfast
steady
stiff
firm
ardent
brawny
robust
sound
sturdy

zealous
distinct
earnest
hale
hardy
mighty
convincing
dependable
reliable
rooted
trustworthy
concrete
fast
secure
constant
equable
fortified
braced
heartened

reinforced
vigorous
vital
spirited
stalwart
energetic
tough
able
durable
virile
athletic
powerful
husky
lusty
brawny
burly
wiry
strapping
rugged

SUCCEED (verb)

fulfill	perform	whip
finish	dominate	outwit
achieve	reap	bend
attain	vanquish	master
gain	out distance	prevail
reach	actualize	triumph
realize	polish off	earn
score	consummation	produce
get	end	yield
arrive at	solve	secure
overcome	get ahead	procure
conquer	prosper	click
beat	thrive	pan out
acquire	complete	go over
win	conclude	catch on
accomplish	surmount	flourish

TO TALK *(verb)*

confer

discuss

utter

chat

converse

talk together

communicate

speak

parley

babble

gab

divulge

spout

banter

verbalize

vocalize

lecture

tell

express

address

debate

commune with

parley

TALK *(noun)*

patter

causerie

prose

negotiation

jargon

interview

utterance

discourse

voice

dialogue

confrontation

parlance

hearsay

oration

sermon

locution

WEALTHY *(adjective)*

opulent
affluent
ample
bounteous
flush
lavish
plentiful
sumptuous
well-to-do
moneyed
comfortable

prosperous
well-off
well-healed
full
fortunate
abounding
abundant
luxuriant
well-fixed
gilded

flourishing
plenteous
bountiful
grandiose
profuse
munificent
lush
luxurious
well-provided-for
resplendent

To order additional copies of **Positive POWERFUL** *Promotional* **Words** or other books by this author, use the handy order form below.

Quantity	Item	Price
	Positive POWERFUL *Promotional* **Words** ($19.95)	
	Creating Special Events ($38.95)	
	Creating Special Events --Audio Cassette ($29.95)	
	Shipping Cost ($3.95 per item)	
	Total Enclosed:	

Kentucky residents add 6% sales tax.

☐ Check or money order enclosed

☐ Mastercard   ☐ Visa

Account #_____Expiration Date_____

Cardholder Signature:_____

Ship to:_____

_____

_____

Phone # (day)_____

For more information, please call or write:

Master Publications, Inc.
10331 Linn Station Road
Louisville, Kentucky 40223
502-426-3021